KU-736-399

In England the years between 1870 and 1885 witnessed a movement that had a long and deeply felt influence on design theory and practice. The Aesthetic Movement produced art and design of unprecedented quality and originality: in architecture, dogmatic Gothic gave way to a functional Queen Anne style; the influence of Japanese art brought a fresh and striking simplicity to interior design, a resurgence of graphic art led to some of the most dazzling work by such children's book illustrators as Randolph Caldecott, Kate Greenaway and Walter Crane; and William Morris's designs for fabrics and furniture revitalized the Victorian interior.

Robin Spencer traces the origins and development of the Movement from its Pre-Raphaelite beginnings to its extension into *fin-de-siècle* Art Nouveau. He clarifies the Aesthetic confusion (from which Whistler more than anyone suffered). For to the Victorian public the lily and the sunflower became the emblems of an Aesthetic reawakening. But such popular manifestations of the Movement were total anathema to serious artists for whom worthwhile artistic endeavour was entirely divorced from ephemeral fashion. Whistler was moved to say: 'Art is upon the Town!—to be chucked under the chin by the passing gallant—to be enticed within the gates of the householder—to be coaxed into company, as a proof of culture and refinement.' Whistler's relationships with Ruskin, the popular Aesthetic Movement and its high priest Oscar Wilde are examined here for the first time, together with several of his previously unpublished designs.

Robin Spencer is Lecturer in the History of Art at the University of St Andrews. He previously held the post of Research Assistant to the Whistler Collections in Glasgow University.

The Aesthetic Movement:

theory and practice

Robin Spencer

General Editor David Herbert

Studio Vista/Dutton Pictureback

Acknowledgements

Apart from the sources listed in the bibliography (see page 155) I have received help, encouragement and advice from several people. I would particularly like to include here and thank Joan Allgrove, Christopher Carter, Mrs Penelope Hotchkis (*née* Ionides), Helen Langdon, Margaret Macdonald, Robin Rennie, Professor John Steer and Professor McLaren Young. Needless to say, none of them can be held responsible for any errors of fact or judgement which appear in the text. My greatest debt of gratitude however is to my wife Isobel, who has not only discussed the book with me at every stage but has also, on her weekly visits to Glasgow, transported home many useful books—some of them exceptionally heavy—so that I could further my research.

I am also grateful for the photographic skills of Philip Mann, Peter Adamson and his assistant John Stevenson, as well as the invaluable secretarial help of Joan Patrick; all, with the exception of Philip Mann, of the University of St Andrews.

© Robin Spencer 1972
Designed by Ian Craig
Published in Great Britain by Studio Vista
Blue Star House, Highgate Hill, London N19
and in the United States of America by E. P. Dutton and Co., Inc.
201 Park Avenue South, New York, NY10003
Set in 11 pt Bembo
Made and printed in Great Britain
by Richard Clay (The Chaucer Press) Ltd, Bungay, Suffolk

ISBN 0 289 70111 2 (paperback)
ISBN 0 289 70112 0 (hardback)

Contents

The cover is based on Walter Crane's design for the jacket of *A Floral Fantasy in an Old English Garden* published by Harper and Brothers 1898

Edward Burne-Jones *Pygmalion and the Image I, The Heart Desires* 1868–
78 Oil on canvas $38\frac{3}{8} \times 29\frac{1}{2}$ in. (97·5 × 74·9 cm)
City Museum and Art Gallery, Birmingham

1 Origins

The Aesthetic Movement was not specially created by artists for artists, and it therefore had no formal organization or manifesto. Its roots cannot be traced to one artistic innovation or a single painting, as is the case with many twentieth-century art movements from Cubism onwards. Contrary to the claims of its advocates, the Aesthetic Movement did not remain the property of a progressive few, for at its height in the mid-1880s it was enjoyed by several levels of society, from the Prince of Wales to the middle classes. If you were rich and 'enlightened' or on the fringe of certain artistic circles, you might live in a Norman Shaw house, commission William Morris to design original furniture, and own paintings by Whistler; but if this was not within reach, a fabric from Liberty's, a Japanese screen and an armful of peacock feathers would do just as well and were more easily obtained. There were thus differing degrees of 'aesthetic awareness', but as the Movement was satirized as a whole, the individual contributions of serious painters and designers were—and still are—confused in the public's mind. These very ideas of taste, good or bad, exist today on coffee tables in the Ideal Homes of those whom the main artistic achievements of the twentieth century have passed by: and the recent revival of William Morris's wallpaper designs, for very much the same sort of clientèle as that of a hundred years ago, might well be argued as the legacy of one of the few art movements supported by the middle classes.

The fact that there were no painters or designers of real importance anxious to claim personal responsibility for the Movement left plenty of room for its high priests, from Oscar Wilde down to the anonymous journalists of the Aesthetic fortnightlies. They were the real creators of Aesthetic taste so far as the willing

over page
Joseph Paxton, The Crystal Palace, after its re-erection at Sydenham *c.* 1855
(photo, Victoria and Albert Museum)

public was concerned; and those unwilling to become aesthetes preferred to endorse the sentiments of *Punch*'s caricatures or Gilbert and Sullivan's satire. But the gap between the two camps could at times be extremely narrow; for in spite of its satirical content, Gilbert and Sullivan's comic opera *Patience* (to take only one example) was so popular that it too became part of the Aesthetic cult, and its librettist, W.S.Gilbert, even lived in a 'Queen Anne style' house. These apparent inconsistencies invite the attention of a social historian, but they also underline the paradox of an age which produced not only a vogue in Art Industry to appeal to the fashion-conscious middle-class consumer, but also, and more significantly, painting and applied art which, at its best, was to influence design reform and artistic autonomy in the twentieth century.

The theory behind the art of the Aesthetic Movement was that it could be enjoyed for its own sake, and need impart nothing more than its own decorative existence to the beholder. This idea, breaking down the barriers between graphic art and painting, also helped design to climb from its long-held position of inferiority to challenge the fine arts of painting, sculpture and architecture, and attempt to co-operate with them on mutual terms.

The Movement thus arose partly in reaction to the immediate past, dominated by serious-minded, rule-book Gothic architects, and the overloaded sentiment of literary-minded, morally-conscious Victorian painters. The classic battle for the stylistic supremacy of Gothic or Greek was eventually replaced by a preference for domestic Dutch and a taste for the art of Japan. These reactions fulfilled the nineteenth century's growing need for freer self-expression and better design standards; for, while its extreme manifestations of whimsical form overlap with the *bizarreries* of Art Nouveau, the functional elegance of its best applied art leads directly to the Modern movement.

Reactions and movements do not occur in a vacuum or spring up unbidden overnight, and the Aesthetic Movement is no exception, for its origins were deeply embedded in mid-nineteenth-century attitudes to art and its role in society. The impetus for the appearance and aesthetics of much British art and design between 1870 and 1885 came from artists who several years before had wrestled quite independently with their own aesthetic and social problems and pursued their own conclusion, oblivious of the Aesthetic publicity which eventually caught them up. The idea behind the more progressive trends in art and design took time to filter through to the general public and the Aesthetic journals; and it is these early beginnings in the 1850s and 1860s which prepared the ground for the Aesthetic Movement.

The 1850s in England saw the victory of Gothic revival architecture as a national building style. Gothic's growing ascendancy over its Roman and Greek rivals had been symbolically established in Britain by A.W.N.Pugin (1812–52) who poured the energies of his short life into the designing of the Houses of Parliament and the setting up of a campaign for the ecclesiastical and architectural principles of the Gothic style. A year before he died Pugin was also responsible for arranging the Medieval Courts of the Great Exhibition in 1851. The Great Exhibition, housed in Joseph Paxton's revolutionary structure of iron and glass, did much to direct the attention of Europe away from France and towards Britain as a design-conscious nation. Yet, in the applied arts, eclecticism was still rampant and, in spite of Prince Albert's and Sir Henry Cole's efforts for quality rather than quantity, most of the objects exhibited in 1851 reveal that Ruskin's exhortations in *The Seven Lamps of Architecture* (1849) for a national style and for a Gothic consistency of ornament had not filtered through to the centres of mass production. 'And Birmingham and Manchester arose in their might—And Art was relegated to the curiosity shop.' So wrote James McNeill Whistler thirty-five years later in his 'Ten O'Clock' lecture.

However, the early 1850s were fruitful for progressive painting. Individual expression had been introduced to the walls of the Royal Academy by the appearance there in 1849 of works by the Pre-Raphaelite Brotherhood. With their admiration for Italian painting before Raphael and a determination to paint only what was true to nature, the main protagonists William Holman Hunt (1827–1910), John Everett Millais (1829–96) and Dante Gabriel Rossetti (1828–82) won the support of the greatest Victorian art critic, John Ruskin. Holman Hunt's *The Awakening Conscience* (Royal Academy 1853) needed Ruskin to explain its

As he that taketh away a garment in cold weather
so is he that singeth songs to an heavy heart.

William Holman Hunt *The Awakening Conscience* 1853
Oil on canvas 29½ × 21⅝ in. (74·9 × 54·9 cm) Trustees of Sir Colin and
Lady Anderson
The quotation on the frame is from Proverbs and the marigolds and
bells are probably emblems of sorrow and warning.

John Everett Millais *Apple Blossoms* (*Spring*) 1859
Oil on canvas $43\frac{1}{2} \times 68$ in. ($110 \cdot 5 \times 172 \cdot 7$ cm) Coll. Lord Leverhulme

moral symbolism to a mystified public; but this painting about the failing of human desire equally emphasized the inadequacy of cheap modern design—witness the nasty veneered piano, the garish fabrics and surrounding gew-gaws. Holman Hunt was the only member of the Pre-Raphaelite Brotherhood to pursue obsessively what he believed to be its original ideas. By the mid-fifties the Brotherhood had disintegrated as a corporate body, and each member went his separate way. Soon Millais abandoned the rigidity of Pre-Raphaelite morality in favour of subjects less polemically demanding, painted in a much freer style. *Apple Blossoms* was eventually shown at the Royal Academy in 1859. It tells no story and has no moral line; in fact this quiet, decorative lyricism would be more at home in the context of the following decade.

Rossetti proved to be the greatest individual of them all, and by far the most influential. As a Pre-Raphaelite in the early fifties he struggled, more or less unsuccessfully, to come to terms with major subject paintings but later in that decade devoted himself

Dante Gabriel Rossetti *The Blue Closet* 1857
Watercolour 13½ × 9¾ in. (34·3 × 24·8 cm) Tate Gallery, London

increasingly to watercolours of intimate subjects from medieval and legendary life. His rich poetic imagination concentrated on themes from Arthurian legend and from Dante: the hypersensitive reaction of the Pre-Raphaelites to brilliant natural colours was channelled towards a mysterious evocation of a past world, without narrative or conventional space, and remote from the realities of mid-Victorian life. Through his friendship with Ruskin and Ford Madox Brown, however, he too had been awakened to the poverty of design in everyday life, and for a period gave a weekly lesson at F.D.Maurice's Working Men's College where Ruskin also taught.

At Oxford, as undergraduates in the 1850s, William Morris (1834–96) and Edward Burne-Jones (1833–98) had been greatly influenced by the ideas of the Pre-Raphaelites; and by 1856 they had both met Rossetti. The decorations for the Oxford Union in 1857 consolidated their youthful enthusiasm for the art of Rossetti who together with Arthur Hughes, Spencer Stanhope and Val Prinsep worked alongside them, but it was not until 1859 that their medieval enthusiasm was realized in a more practical way by the building of the Red House for William Morris and his wife. Philip Webb (1831–1915), the architect, who had known Morris when they worked together in the office of the architect George Edmund Street, conceived the Red House not as an archaeological reproduction in the medieval style but simply as a home, solid and workable, for a newly-married couple who happened to possess a romantic and perhaps idealistic view of the Middle Ages.

It was on this basis, and out of the reformatory character of Ruskin's campaigning, that the firm Morris, Marshall, Faulkner and Company was founded in 1861. Its success was largely due to the versatility of its main practitioners, Brown, Burne-Jones, Morris, Rossetti and Webb; and its significance for nineteenth-century design lay in the relentless pursuit, especially by Morris, of the improvement of design standards in an age of machine-made mass production. The firm designed tapestries and wall-papers, as well as furniture, stained glass and domestic utensils; but it was mainly Morris's zeal and socialist views which won it lasting recognition, long after Rossetti had retired to a world of laudanum-soaked isolation in Chelsea.

The decade 1860 to 1870 was a seminal one in France as well as in England; during these years several old traditions died and some new ones were born. In France the death of Delacroix in 1863 and of Ingres in 1867 finally resolved a conflict which, although never as fierce in the 1860s as in previous decades, had nevertheless split artists and critics into two distinct groups. The controversy had recently been obscured by a new movement which owed little to either Ingres or Delacroix. Realism's greatest exponent in painting was Gustave Courbet and in literature the novelist Champfleury. The new subject matter of everyday life, unidealized and factual, and often with distinctly socialist overtones, awoke the sensibilities of a new generation of critics. Charles Baudelaire provided fresh aesthetic formulation for the celebration of a sophisticated and original Realism in his essay on *The Painter of Modern Life*, published in 1863. Although Baudelaire had in mind the illustrator Constantin Guys, the ideas

Philip Webb, The Red House, Bexleyheath, built for William Morris in 1859
(photo, National Monuments Record)

William Morris & Co., rush-bottomed chair, after 1862
Victoria and Albert Museum, London

Edward Burne-Jones *Chaucer Asleep* for William Morris & Co. 1861/4
Panel of stained glass 17 × 18 in. (43·2 × 45·7 cm) Victoria and Albert
Museum, London

of the essay were extended and transformed in an original way
by Edouard Manet in his painting of elegant Second Empire
Parisian society, *La Musique aux Tuileries*.

The English poet Swinburne was a great admirer of Baudelaire's poetry, and in 1862 wrote the first review in English of
Baudelaire's *Les Fleurs du Mal*. In his turn, although at first
indirectly through Fantin-Latour and Whistler, Baudelaire

Philip Webb, three glasses, for William Morris & Co. 1862
Victoria and Albert Museum, London

praised Swinburne's poem 'August' and expressed the hope that
he would soon meet his English admirer. In fact no such meeting
ever occurred, but their mutual appreciation was a significant
aesthetic bridge between France and England, made doubly so
by the fact that Whistler was the go-between and a regular
visitor to the house in Cheyne Walk, Chelsea, where from 1862
Rossetti and Swinburne lived.

James McNeill Whistler (1834–1903) came to London in 1859, and by 1863 had settled in Chelsea. In 1855 he had left America for Paris where, for a time, he frequented the studios of the English artists' colony which included E.J.Poynter, George du Maurier and Thomas Armstrong, all later to become, in their own respective ways, very much figures of importance in English art. Apart from some valuable lessons in technique learnt at Gleyre's studio (where Monet, Renoir, Sisley and Bazille met six years later) the greatest impact on Whistler in Paris was the art of Courbet. His portraits shared Courbet's proletarian subject-matter and a Realist's admiration for seventeenth-century Dutch and Spanish art. Courbet had personally praised Whistler's *At the Piano* when it was exhibited in Bonvin's studio in 1859, and when Whistler came to London in the same year he was confident of success. In 1861 Millais described Whistler's Rembrandt-like *La Mère Gérard* as 'the finest piece of colour that has been on the walls of the Royal Academy for years'.

Whistler too saw a similar quality in the work of Millais, and he confided to his friend Fantin-Latour that Millais's *The Eve of St Agnes* (Royal Academy 1863) was a 'truly great painting'. *The Eve of St Agnes* depicts a female figure lit by a solitary shaft of light, standing in a sumptuously decorated interior. But Whistler's admiration was aroused not so much by the nature of its Keatsian mythology (a *poésie* not found in Courbet's art) as by the richness of colour and design. Had he been more willing to meet mid-Victorian taste, Whistler might not have made *The White Girl* such an uncompromisingly Realist painting and it might have found its way into the Royal Academy (where it was rejected in 1862) rather than the Salon des Refusées where in 1863, together with Manet's *Déjeuner sur l'herbe* (then called *Le Bain*), it attracted so much controversial attention.

By 1863 Whistler was on close terms with the eccentric Swinburne–Rossetti household, and had assimilated most of what he found interesting in English art (see page 25). He was so impressed with Rossetti that he persuaded Fantin-Latour to include him in the group painting *Hommage à Delacroix* (in which Whistler figures so prominently), but in the end Rossetti was unable to be present for the sittings. Rossetti had admired the direction in which Whistler appeared to be moving although he was unable

James McNeill Whistler *La Mère Gérard* 1858
Oil on canvas 12 × 8½ in. (30·5 × 21·6 cm) Coll. Bernard Solomon,
Los Angeles (photo, Malcolm Lubliner)
The painting was originally in the collection of A.C.Swinburne to
whom it was given by the artist.

John Everett Millais *The Eve of St Agnes* 1863
Oil on canvas $46\frac{1}{2} \times 61$ in. ($118 \cdot 1 \times 154 \cdot 9$ cm) Coll. H.M.Queen Elizabeth, the Queen Mother
Exhibited at the Royal Academy 1863 with a quotation from Keats's poem.

James McNeill Whistler *The White Girl* 1862
Oil on canvas $84\frac{1}{2} \times 42\frac{1}{2}$ in. ($214 \cdot 6 \times 108$ cm) National Gallery of Art, Washington DC, Harris Whittemore Collection
Whistler later retitled the painting *Symphony in White No. I: The White Girl*

to appreciate really progressive French painting when he visited Manet's Paris studio in November 1864. Whistler, on the other hand, was well informed of the conversations at the Café de Bade and, if he was not present himself, he kept in constant touch through his correspondence and friendship with Fantin.

In London in the sixties Whistler did not share the feeling for reform which inspired the members of Morris's firm. He was

James McNeill Whistler *Symphony in White No. II: The Little White Girl* 1864
Oil on canvas 30 × 20½ in. (76·2 × 52·1 cm) Tate Gallery, London
Exhibited at the Royal Academy 1865 with Swinburne's verses 'Before the Mirror' pasted on the frame.

Dante Gabriel Rossetti *Lady in Yellow* 1863
Pencil and watercolour 16 × 12 in. (40·6 × 30·5 cm) Tate Gallery,
London

Jean Auguste Dominique Ingres *L'Age d'Or* 1862
Oil on paper pasted on panel 18¼ × 24¼ in. (46·4 × 61·6 cm) Fogg Art
Museum, Cambridge, Mass. Grenville Winthrop Bequest
A reduced replica of the scheme originally planned for the Château de
Dampierre.

much more concerned with his own painting problems than with
pseudo-medievalizing or the state of British design; and Morris's
attitudinizing socialism was, and always remained, utterly repug-
nant to him. Instead he evolved a system of abstract nomencla-
ture suggested by music; he renamed the portraits of his Irish
mistress Joanna Hiffernan, *Symphony in White No. I : The White
Girl*, and *Symphony in White No. II : The Little White Girl*, etc. By
1867 he had radically rethought his own art. His painting relied
first on the inclusion of the brilliant colours, fans and costumes
found in Oriental art; and, as the series of 'White Girls' progressed, even the spatial sophistication of Japanese prints began
to dominate his pictorial schemes.

LE REPOS

Puvis de Chavannes *Le Repos* 1863
Oil on canvas 42¾ × 58¼ in. (108·6 × 148 cm) National Gallery of **Art,**
Washington DC, Widener Collection

Swinburne had written a series of verses, 'Before the Mirror',
for *The Little White Girl* and both he and Rossetti had been
'stunned' by the painting. It is probably more than accidental
that the carefully orchestrated arrangement of a girl wistfully
gazing at her own image reminds us of Ingres's portrait of the
Comtesse d'Haussonville. Ingres's reputation and influence under-
went a serious reappraisal in the 1860s, especially when after his
death in 1867 a great retrospective exhibition was mounted in
Paris. This had affected artists in both France and England, not
least Whistler who, in 1867, although admitting that he did not
go into raptures in front of Ingres's painting and allowing that
his style was not at all Greek, nevertheless wished that Ingres had

Frederick Walker *Bathers* 1867
Oil on canvas $36\frac{1}{2} \times 84\frac{1}{2}$ in. (92·7 × 214·6 cm) Trustees of the Lady
Lever Art Gallery, Port Sunlight

been his master rather than Courbet. Even earlier Fantin too had
mentioned that he had little patience with Manet and Baudelaire
because they were inclined to dismiss Ingres altogether.

In France, Puvis de Chavannes (1824–98) was creating in his
work an antique world of allegorical legend, just as unreal as
Rossetti's painting was in England. His work claimed the attention of Parisian critics when *Concordia* and *Bellum* were exhibited
in the Salon of 1861, and *Le Travail* and *Le Repos* in 1863. His
subjects evoke a sort of Golden Age idyll, which the symbolists
loved so much twenty years later, but which, in historical terms,
links him directly with Ingres's Golden Age decorations begun

The towel held by the central figure was added later at the request of the first owner William Graham.

for the Duc de Luynes at the Château de Dampierre in 1843 but abandoned in 1850. The formula of naked nymphs disporting in woodland glades and sunning themselves by water was, of course, in the great classical tradition; but to any inventive artist, whether French or English, it was a theme capable of endless variation. Frederick Walker (1840–75) produced a not dissimilar kind of *frisson* with his *Bathers* (Royal Academy 1867) but his advanced style of naturalism (a 7 ft canvas painted principally out of doors) owes more to Pre-Raphaelite techniques and a first-hand knowledge of the Elgin Marbles than it does to the French classical tradition.

There were many artists in England who, at one time or another in the sixties, were affected by what was clearly a classical revival. Subjects did not have to be remote, but 'remoteness' and if possible an 'other-worldly' atmosphere were essential to their success. Frederick Leighton (1830–96) painted subjects from the mythological past, such as *Orpheus and Eurydice* (1864). Thomas Armstrong (1832–1911) became the Director of the South Kensington Museum in 1881, but in the sixties after a period of study in France and Belgium he painted a number of melancholic compositions often consisting of ladies in marble halls playing

Thomas Armstrong *Haytime* 1869
Oil on canvas $49\frac{3}{4} \times 61\frac{7}{8}$ in. (126·4 × 157·2 cm) Victoria and Albert Museum, London

Albert Moore *The Marble Seat* 1865
Oil on canvas 29 × 18½ in. (152·4 × 47 cm) present whereabouts unknown

lyres. His *Haytime* (Royal Academy 1869) is devoid of obvious classical references, and its sweet nostalgia—far from the hardships of real agricultural labour—is evoked instead by a gentle colour harmony of greens and violets.

The greatest *Ingriste* in England was undoubtedly Albert Moore (1841–93). The son of a north country portrait painter, he came to London in 1858. As a member of the group at the Royal Academy Schools which included Fred Walker, Henry Holiday and William Blake Richmond, Moore applied his precocious talents to works which almost outpainted the Pre-Raphaelites for 'truth to nature'. A trip to Europe in the company of the young architect William Eden Nesfield in 1859 opened his eyes to the art of the past, and especially to Roman painting at Pompeii and Herculaneum. He was well prepared to assimilate the Elgin Marbles which, in 1865, had undergone restoration and rearrangement in the Elgin Room at the British Museum.

In 1865 he exhibited at the Royal Academy *The Marble Seat*

James McNeill Whistler *Symphony in White No. III* 1867
Oil on canvas 20½ × 30⅛ in. (57·2 × 76·5 cm) Barber Institute of Fine
Arts, University of Birmingham
Begun in 1865 and completed in 1867.

Edouard Manet *Le Repos* (Berthe Morisot) *c.* 1870
Oil on canvas 58⅛ × 44½ in. (173 × 113 cm) Museum of Art, Rhode
Island School of Design

which was actually noted by one critic for its resemblance to the
Elgin Marbles. *The Marble Seat* is a sort of *Déjeuner sur l'herbe*
with an Anglo-Greek accent, but Baudelaire would surely have
disapproved, for its subject is clearly *la vie grècque* rather than *la
vie moderne*. On the other hand, Whistler must have admired it
enormously, for it inaugurated a close formal interdependence
between the two men that lasted until 1870.

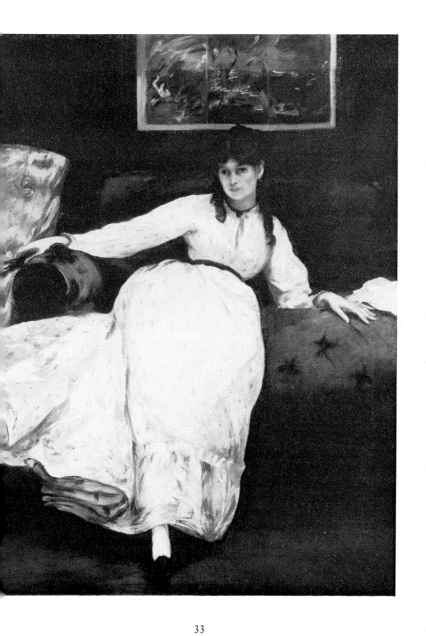

Albert Moore *Pomegranates* 1866
Oil on canvas 14 × 10 in. (35·6 × 25·4 cm) Courtesy of the Guildhall Art Gallery, London

Moore's *Pomegranates*, shown at the Royal Academy in 1866, is really Poussin's *Et in Arcadia Ego* transferred to a Victorian Design Centre interior; and soon afterwards Whistler (whose *japonisme* greatly appealed to Moore) translated the motif of three very similar semi-classical females to the spaceless anonymity of a Japanese print in *Pink and Grey: Three Figures*. This may well have had its effect on advanced art circles in Paris as well, for after his visit to London in 1869 Edouard Manet's painting reveals a concern for similar aesthetic problems.

Pink and Grey: Three Figures, which Whistler sometimes referred to as his *Symphony in White No. IV*, was part of a decorative scheme of six paintings planned for his Liverpool patron F.R.Leyland. The *Three Figures* painting was the only one enlarged, but clearly Whistler already had an eye to creating a

James McNeill Whistler *Pink and Grey: Three Figures* 1868
Oil on canvas 54¾ × 73 in. (139·1 × 185·4 cm) Tate Gallery, London

major decorative scheme, and the so-called 'Six Projects' are a
direct forerunner of the famous Peacock Room painted for
Leyland six years later. It was the 'Six Projects' on which the
poet-aesthetician Swinburne concentrated when he wrote a
review of Whistler's work in 1868. Swinburne included in his
review an appreciation of the work of Albert Moore as well as
that of Burne-Jones; and he made it clear that, although his
readers would not find this sort of work on the walls of the
Royal Academy, these artists were, nevertheless, producing the
most modern, original and important work in London at the
time. Swinburne saw in Albert Moore's painting a direct link
with the theory of art for art's sake, and identified Moore's work
with the source of that philosophy: 'His painting is to artists
what the verse of Théophile Gautier is to the poets, the faultless

Edward William Godwin, buffet, 1877
Victoria and Albert Museum, London
First designed for himself in 1867.

and secure expression of an exclusive worship of things formally beautiful.' He was also anxious, in the passages devoted to Whistler, to explain the philosophy of beauty for beauty's sake; and a consequence of this was that the subject, which existed in its own right and for its own sake only, must never reveal how it achieved its being or show the hand of the creator. Thus, to Swinburne, Whistler's 'Six Projects' 'seem to have grown as a flower grows, not in any forcing house of ingenious and laborious cunning'. In a series of Propositions in 1886, issued as a kind of postscript to the 'Ten O'Clock' lecture, Whistler, who by that time was being blamed for every aesthetic aberration not committed by Oscar Wilde, stated: 'The masterpiece should appear as the flower to the painter—perfect in its bud as in its bloom—with no reason to explain its presence—no mission to fulfil—a joy to the artist.'

The seeds of Whistler's brown paper pamphlet dialectic and the ideas behind the 'Ten O'Clock' lecture were already sown in the mid-sixties, and Swinburne's influence on Whistler then was exceptionally formative. Swinburne helped provide him with the early basis on which to build his case for the prosecution in the libel action brought against Ruskin in 1878; and the establishment of a close aesthetic relationship between Swinburne, Whistler and Albert Moore helps to put into context Moore's support of Whistler's art at the Ruskin trial and the subsequent dedication by Whistler of his first pamphlet *Whistler versus Ruskin; Art and Art Critics* to Moore.

In the meantime in the sixties the cult of the beautiful for a time threatened to turn into a cult of Venus. In 1868 Burne-Jones began a series of four paintings based on the story of Pygmalion, a Cyprian sculptor who created an image so beautiful that he fell in love with it and had it turned into real life by the goddess Aphrodite. The subject was treated in verse by William Morris in *The Earthly Paradise*. The idea is really a Pre-Raphaelite one, because it is about the whole problem of truth to nature; but the idea of imitating something in such a realistic way that it comes to life takes the Pre-Raphaelite ideal of truth to nature to extremes. Burne-Jones explains the situation in a narrative progression from the sculptor's contemplation (*The Heart Desires*) to the adoration of the living flesh (*The Soul Attains*), by means of some

Albert Moore *Venus* 18
Oil on canvas 62 × 28
(157·5 × 71·1 cm)
City of York Art Galle

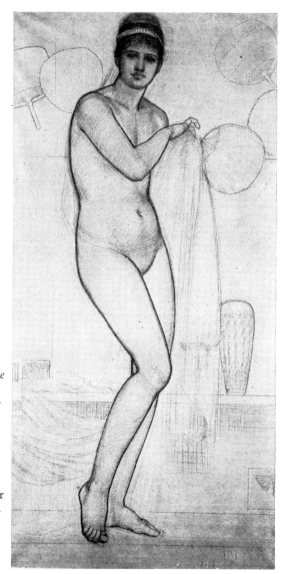

James McNeill Whistler
Cartoon for a Venus Figure
1869
Pencil (with pricked out-
line) 47 × 24$\frac{3}{16}$ in.
(119·4 × 69·2 cm)
Courtesy of the Smith-
sonian Institution, Freer
Gallery of Art,
Washington DC
It is recorded that Whistler
had completed a *Venus* in
time for the Royal
Academy exhibition of
1870. No such painting
was ever shown.

Over page James McNeill Whistler *Symphony in Blue and Pink* 1868
Oil on prepared academy board, mounted on wood panel 18$\frac{3}{8}$ × 24$\frac{3}{8}$ in.
(46·7 × 61·9 cm) Courtesy of the Smithsonian Institution, Freer Gallery
of Art, Washington DC
One of the *Six Projects*.

quattrocento Rossettian architecture. Obviously Burne-Jones was at pains to say something original and important about Beauty. However, the finished product was as ludicrous in 1879 (when the series was exhibited at the Grosvenor Gallery) as it is today; for, apart from the whole idea being taken too seriously, the series relies too much on the traditional concept of narrative, setting the figures in a definite time and place. This makes it difficult for us to concentrate on the Timelessness usually associated with Beauty in an Ideal situation. The series also points to the limitations of Pre-Raphaelite convention and is a salutary memorial to its often over-serious endeavour. In contrast with Burne-Jones, Albert Moore concentrated on the essentials of Beauty in his *Venus*, exhibited at the Royal Academy in 1869. The background is described by elegant bands of harmonious muted greens and blues, but, except for a bit of drapery, some flowers and a blue and white pot, this nineteenth-century Venus de Milo is quite alone; or, as Swinburne would have said, her reason for being is to be.

Whistler was amazed by Moore's *Venus* and immediately set out to emulate it, but his efforts never got beyond the cartoon stage. By this time Whistler had already begun to realize that his own work too closely resembled that of his friend. In 1870 he even asked the architect, William Eden Nesfield, to supply an impartial judgement as to whether their similarity might be a source of public confusion. In fact, for several years, critics, besides Swinburne, had grouped Whistler's paintings with those by Moore. It was not so much the physical similarity which worried Whistler but the 'general sentiment' they shared. Nesfield made a very tactful reply, admitting the two artists' mutual appreciation, but pointing out their individual qualities. Albert Moore was happy to continue painting classically-draped, languid female figures, singly, in pairs or in groups, until his death in 1893. But for Whistler, it was obviously quite useless for two artists to go on duplicating the same 'sentiment'. Although he never abandoned altogether the Graeco-Japanese themes of the sixties, Whistler, within a matter of months, began painting the Nocturnes, and returned to the Thames, a subject which had preoccupied him when he first arrived in London in 1859.

2 The 1870s: 'Queen Anne style' architecture and the influence of Japan

George Edmund Street (1824–81) was one of the most prolific and resourceful practitioners of the Gothic Revival style in the second half of the nineteenth century. His office in the fifties and sixties was an attractive proposition for a young aspiring architect, and it was there that Richard Norman Shaw (1831–1912) succeeded Philip Webb as chief draughtsman in 1858. Much of Shaw's early work after leaving Street's office was done in collaboration with William Eden Nesfield (1835–88) with whom he set up a partnership in 1862.

Nesfield was in the van of progressive artists and designers who knew Swinburne. The Jewish painter Simeon Solomon had introduced him to the poet as early as 1863 and Solomon was also a great admirer of Nesfield's Japanese *objets d'art*. Touches of *japonisme* in the form of lotus-flower friezes appeared in some of Nesfield's early buildings such as Cloverley Hall in Shropshire and Coombe Abbey, Warwickshire, both built in 1862. It was through his friendship with Nesfield that Albert Moore secured several commissions to decorate the interiors of a number of churches and country houses, including Coombe; and he had already gained a considerable reputation as a mural painter before Whistler met him in 1865. William Lock Eastlake wrote the first *History of the English Gothic Revival*, published in 1872, and in it advocated this very sort of co-operation, by underlining the advantages to a Gothic house-holder of giving work to artists like Henry Stacy Marks, Henry Holiday or Albert Moore 'to enliven every room in his house with pictured allegory or old-world lore'. But in the decade in which the *History of the English Gothic Revival* appeared, new partnerships in the field of architecture and interior design had arisen to take the place of those suggested by Eastlake.

The 'Queen Anne style' of architecture which emerged in domestic building in London in the mid-seventies is inevitably associated with the work of Richard Norman Shaw, but seventeenth-century Dutch motifs had already appeared in Nesfield's house,

William Eden Nesfield, The Golden Lodge, Kinmel Park, Denbighshire, 1866–8 (photo, National Monuments Record)
Note the sunflower decoration on the frieze and over the dormer window.

Richard Norman Shaw, New Zealand Chambers, Leadenhall Street, London, 1872
(photo, National Monuments Record)

Kinmel Park, Abergele, Denbighshire, in 1866–8, and it is more likely that the formation of the 'Queen Anne style' was a result of collaboration between Nesfield and Shaw in the later sixties and early seventies. Its main characteristics were established by 1872 with Shaw's designs for New Zealand Chambers in Leadenhall Street; but the real meaning of the style was best suited to the houses which Shaw built in Chelsea, Cheyne House (1875–6)

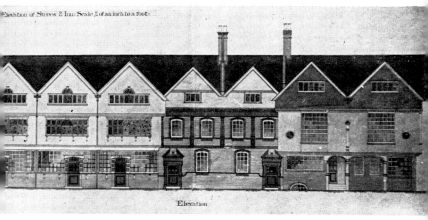

Elevation

Richard Norman Shaw, *The Tabard Inn and Stores*, Bedford Park, 1877
Pencil and watercolour 17¾ × 37¼ in. (45·1 × 94·6 cm) Victoria and
Albert Museum, London

Richard Norman Shaw, Old Swan House, Chelsea, 1876–7
(photo, National Monuments Record)

and Old Swan House (1876–7). In the decade that saw the rising
of Street's Law Courts, Shaw's refined, unadorned elevations
were revolutionary indeed. The attenuated fenestration and high
gables do not conform to any dogmatic system of decoration,
and owe nothing to the Gothic past. The detailing is plain and
crisp, offering wide scope for a picturesque grouping of solids
and voids. Shaw practised this basic vocabulary in various buildings in Hampstead, in his own house of 1875, and in one designed
for Kate Greenaway ten years later.

The essential quality of Shaw's architecture was its basic
domesticity, its human scale and its renunciation of impractical
Gothic for a more comfortable and practical home environment.
In addition to the houses which Shaw projected for practising
artists, he also provided homes for the sort of people W.S.Gilbert
and George du Maurier satirized in the early eighties. The Bedford Park scheme was the idea of a property speculator, Jonathan
Carr, who in 1877 employed Shaw to build a whole suburbia of

Owen Jones, wallpaper printed by John Trumble & Co. 1858
Victoria and Albert Museum, London

cottage-villas for the middle classes. Shaw's designs, quaint and
'olde-worlde', were a conscious (if not self-conscious) attempt to
provide a vernacular, almost bijou backdrop out of the half-
timbered elements of old cottage architecture; and as a result,
attracted many of those who were 'aesthetically aware'. The use
of red brick rather than dressed stone became more and more
common in an age which witnessed a domestic revival.

Shaw's Bedford Park utopia was not, however, without its
critics, and William Morris was one who disapproved of such
fanciful eclecticism. In 1874 Morris had set up in business on his
own and soon after began to devote a lot of his time to lectures
and socialist theories. His primary concern was for an art of high-
quality craftsmanship that could be put within the reach of every-
one; and this socialist programme combined with his vigorous
attacks on contemporary design methods make him an important

Albert Moore, wallpaper printed by Jeffrey & Co. 1860s (?)
Victoria and Albert Museum, London (photo, Philip Mann)

figure for the twentieth, as well as the nineteenth century. But, it must be admitted, *News from Nowhere* (1890), which describes an imaginary other-world paradise suitable for William Morris-type activity, reads more convincingly as a literary utopia than as a blue-print for any real future existence. In a lecture given in 1878 entitled 'The Lesser Arts', Morris stated in systematic fashion his views on the future of the applied arts, and set out to establish the Decorative Arts on equal footing with Painting, Sculpture and Architecture. His main argument for this was based on the relationship between history and decoration: 'So strong is the bond between history and decoration that in the practice of the latter we cannot, if we would, wholly shake off the influence of past times over what we do at present.' In many ways, statements like this show Morris as a figure very much of his own time and help to explain why, as a would-be

William Morris, 'Trellis' wallpaper printed by Jeffrey & Co. 1862
Victoria and Albert Museum, London
One of Morris's first wallpapers. The birds were drawn by Philip Webb.

architect, he first articled himself to the main-line Gothic designer Street.

Morris's designs also acknowledged a debt to the art of the past, but in this he was by no means the only design-conscious reformer working at the time. Some of his early patterns share marked similarities with the wallpaper designs of Owen Jones (1809–74). Jones, a designer and reformer in his own right, also published a lavishly chromolithographed volume, *The Grammar of Ornament*, in 1856, which includes an entire vocabulary of patterns and motifs from many different cultures and civilizations, from textiles to mosaics. It may not have encouraged originality in the hands of an uninspired eclectic; but Morris's achievement was that he saw beyond Jones and developed much bolder, more consistent ways of expressing the richness and diversity of what was best in the history of the decorative arts.

After about 1876 Morris's designs take on a greater formality and are less obviously derived from natural forms. Again, it would seem that this change is due to Morris looking at the art of the past, for about this time he became interested in weaving techniques and discovered Italian Renaissance textiles together with their stylistic antecedents in the South Kensington Museum.

William Morris's contribution to design is essentially in the Western tradition, and his own Arts and Crafts movement remains relatively unaffected by the fashion for Japanese art and design. However, it is interesting to see that in the late sixties Murray Marks, who was an early collector of 'blue and white' china and Japanese prints, proposed to start a Fine Art Company with Alexander Ionides, Rossetti, Burne-Jones and Morris as shareholders. Their intention was to market prints, china, paintings by Burne-Jones and Rossetti, as well as etchings by Whistler. Little is heard again of these activities, but the company's one-time existence provides a useful connecting commentary on the advanced compositional aesthetics of Whistler in the late sixties and seventies, and the equally innovatory motifs behind the Arts and Crafts movement, for which Morris was mainly responsible.

Sir Rutherford Alcock (1809–97) had provided the British public with its first glimpse of the art of Japan at the International Exhibition of 1862. Alcock had been the first representative of

William Morris, 'Bird Pattern', woven textile for Kelmscott House 1879–80 Victoria and Albert Museum, London

North Italian silk, early fifteenth century
Victoria and Albert Museum, London

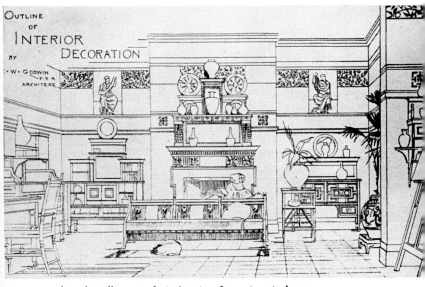

Edward William Godwin 'Design for an interior' 1882
From *The British Architect*, July 1882

William Burges, cabinet, 1858. Painted decoration by E.J.Poynter.
Victoria and Albert Museum, London

the British Crown at Yedo from 1859, and in 1868 wrote a comprehensive account of Japanese artistic practice, with precise details of colour techniques and aspects of Oriental working methods. His *Capital of the Tycoon* (1863) was one of the first publications to contain authentic reproductions of Japanese woodcuts; and the Japanese prints introduced to Europe in the early sixties were soon assimilated into the currents of aesthetic thought by critics, Dante Gabriel's brother William Michael Rossetti in England, and Ernest Chesneau in France.

An appreciation of this kind of art was not completely incompatible with a Gothic temperament. The architect William Burges, remembered most for his extravagant medieval architecture and furnishings, was an early collector of Japanese prints, and Ruskin too shared Rossetti's enthusiasm for them. E.W.Godwin (1833–86), who worked with Burges, also formed a Japanese

Edward William Godwin *Elevation for the White House c.* 1877
Birnie Philip Bequest, University of Glasgow

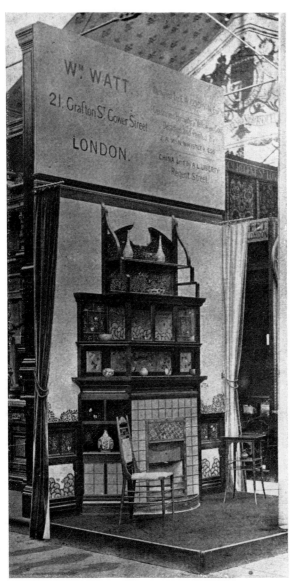

Stand at the Paris Exposition Universelle 1878
Furniture designed by E.W.Godwin, painted by Whistler, and marketed
by William Watt. China lent by Liberty, Regent Street.

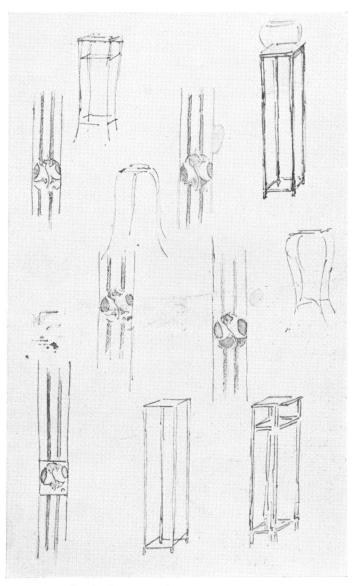

James McNeill Whistler *Designs for Furniture c.* 1878
Pen 7 × 4½ in. (17·8 × 11·4 cm) Birnie Philip Bequest, University of
Glasgow

collection—and was an admirer of Ruskin's architectural theories (his first major success in 1861—the design for the Northampton Town Hall—reflects a close understanding of the Italian Gothic architecture advocated by Ruskin in the *Stones of Venice*, 1851–3). By the mid-sixties Godwin was on close terms with Whistler. Like Whistler and Albert Moore, he was an admirer of Greek as well as Japanese art, and in some of his designs for interiors proved that an admiration for both cultures was not mutually exclusive. His Anglo-Japanese furniture, especially the buffet for the Earl of Limerick at Dromore Castle (see page 36), first made in 1867, is among the most sophisticated of all nineteenth-century designs, and was only surpassed later in the century by the attenuated elegance of the work of the Scottish architect and designer Charles Rennie Mackintosh. Its combination of low vertical and horizontal members in ebonized wood with a leather paper decoration is expressed with the extreme economy found only in Japanese art. It is closest in spirit to Whistler's own paintings in the late sixties, and reflects, even though in a different medium, the same sort of aesthetic.

A vogue for decorated furniture and painted cabinets sprang up in the seventies and made popular a trend begun by the Pre-Raphaelites. This type of 'Art Furniture' was produced—probably in a severely limited edition—when Godwin designed a cabinet which Whistler decorated, not with the representational elements found on commercially manufactured furniture, such as female figures, but with a harmony in yellow and gold. Godwin's furniture, which was probably intended for Whistler's own use in the White House, was exhibited in Paris in 1878 and marketed by William Watt. From this time, date several designs for furniture by Whistler himself; and again, like Godwin ten years before, their elongated character anticipates Art Nouveau and the Glasgow style of the nineties.

Godwin's architecture in the seventies and eighties was quite as advanced as his interior designs, and in 1876 he worked on the Bedford Park project until his designs met with so much criticism that Norman Shaw was appointed in his place. Like Shaw, Godwin built a number of houses and studios for artists, the most notable being those in Tite Street, Chelsea. They seem more solid and compositionally varied than the rather attenuated

Chelsea houses by Shaw of the mid-seventies; but they do have Shaw's high-stepping gables and other features of the Queen Anne style. Probably the most important and certainly the most controversial of Godwin's Tite Street houses was the White House designed for Whistler in 1877–8, but where Whistler left off and Godwin began is not clear, as both men worked very closely on the project. It is certain, however, that the elevation as published in the *British Architect* in 1878 did not wholly represent their intentions. What Whistler required was a house with a comfortable but sparsely-furnished interior in the Japanese style and a small theatre and spacious studio suitable for opening as an atelier to his increasing circle of young artist-admirers. Neither Godwin nor Whistler wanted any exterior decoration in the form of bas-relief sculpture. However, the Metropolitan Board of Works, unsympathetic to their unadorned aesthetic purism, demanded that some token of sculpted decoration should appear; and there ensued a long, tedious and often acrimonious correspondence between the architects and the public authority. As economy also dictated the designers' plans, the employment of a distinguished sculptor of Whistler's own choice such as Sir Edgar Joseph Boehm was quite out of the question, and ultimately a compromise—unsatisfactory to both parties—had to be reached. The demands Whistler made upon the Board of Works in 1878, which had still to emerge from the Pugin era, were extreme; and this head-on clash was not repeated in the case of clients satisfied by more modest aesthetic ambitions.

Thomas Jeckyll (1827–81) was an architect and interior designer who, like his friend Godwin, was able to provide furniture in the Japanese style. He had worked as an architect with the Norwich firm Barnard, Bishop and Barnard, noted for their decorative wrought-iron work. During his lifetime Jeckyll went on to produce some of the most original essays in this medium, incorporating the sunflower motif, which became a popular symbol of the Aesthetic Movement. In 1872 he designed some very individual furniture for Ken Hill, a house built by J.J.Stevenson, and his work fits well in an interior which contains paintings by Thomas Armstrong. A little later, Jeckyll built an extension to No. 1 Holland Park, a house originally designed by Webb. The owner was the Greek Consul-General

Thomas Jeckyll *Sunflower c.* 1876
Wrought iron, made by Barnard, Bishop and Barnard
Victoria and Albert Museum, London

Thomas Jeckyll, dressing-table 1875
Coll. Mrs P.Hotchkis (photo, Peter Adamson)

Porch of No. 1 Holland Park, tiled by William De Morgan *c.* 1888
Wrought-ironwork by Jeckyll (?) (photo, Coll. Mrs P.Hotchkis)

William De Morgan, tile for No. 1 Holland Park *c.* 1888
6 × 6 in. (15·2 × 15·2 cm) Coll. Mrs P.Hotchkis

and financier, Alexander Ionides, who was a friend and patron
to many modern artists. Jeckyll's extension consisted of several
rooms, including a billiard hall hung with Japanese panels of the
Hokusai school. Ionides had an important collection of modern
paintings which included works by Rossetti, Burne-Jones,
Frederick Walker, Frederick Sandys, Whistler and many more;
and for his Holland Park house he commissioned some of the
best interior designers. William De Morgan tiled a porch in
brilliant blues and greens using a natural plant form as a motif.

over page
Dining room at No. 1 Holland Park (photo, Coll. Mrs P.Hotchkis)
Woodwork designed by Philip Webb, silvered ceiling and frieze by
Walter Crane. Note the painted motifs on the door and Whistler's self-
portrait of 1872 (see page 94).

William Morris *The Forest* 1887
4 × 15 ft. (121·9 × 457 cm) Victoria and Albert Museum, London
Woven for Alexander Ionides. Verdure design by Morris, animals by
Philip Webb.

Walter Crane later covered the ceiling and frieze of the dining
room with silver gilt paper and in another room constructed an
ingenious overmantel with gold-backed niches to show Ionides's
collection of Tanagra statuettes to its best advantage. And
Morris, Burne-Jones and Webb were all employed at one time
or another to provide chairs, curtains and tapestries. Of all the
furniture, Jeckyll's is probably the most individual. When
Alexander Ionides was married in 1875 Jeckyll made him a bed-
room suite consisting of wardrobe, dressing-table and commodes.
The furniture was not perhaps as uncompromisingly Japanese as
Godwin's for it retained more conventional Western idioms of
form instead of the subtle interplay of solids and voids found for
instance in Godwin's Dromore buffet. But the detailing, especially the fluted grooved borders, the combination of light-toned
and ebonized woods, and the lacquer panels all betray a distinct
Oriental flavour. The border grooving in particular is very close
in feeling to the decoration Whistler painted on the frames of
his pictures, a practice that he adopted in 1864. Rossetti, Holman
Hunt and Millais had been decorating frames for almost as long
as they had been Pre-Raphaelites, but the motifs they used were
primarily intended to convey a symbolic or religious meaning.
Whistler was a genuine admirer of Jeckyll's talents, and it was
Jeckyll's elaborate interior, the dining room at 49 Princes Gate,
which inspired him in 1876 to make the scheme even more
lavish by creating for its owner, F.R.Leyland, a 'Harmony in

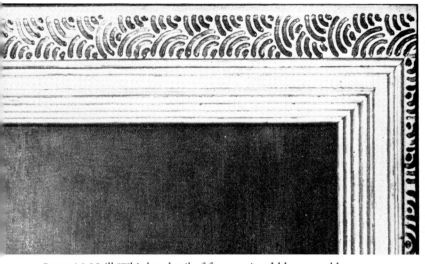

James McNeill Whistler, detail of frame painted blue on gold
Birnie Philip Bequest, University of Glasgow

Thomas Jeckyll, wardrobe (detail) 1875
Coll. Mrs P.Hotchkis (photo, Peter Adamson)

Blue and Gold'. Jeckyll had covered parts of the wall surface with an intricate system of shelves on spindled supports against a background of Spanish leather. Whistler's decoration was based on the eye and tail-feathers of the peacock itself, and he painted the harmony round the entire room, over doors, wall and window shutters. On a blank stretch of wall he painted a decorative panel of two gold peacocks on the blue ground to face one of his own first essays in the Japanese taste, the *Princesse du Pays de la Porcelaine* which hung over the fireplace at the opposite end of the room.

The peacock with its luxurious plumage, like the sunflower, became one of the most popular manifestations of the Aesthetic Movement. It had actually existed in reality as a post-Pre-Raphaelite motif for Rossetti who kept peacocks in an exotic menagerie at his Chelsea house in the 1860s. Albert Moore used the peacock motif exclusively in his interior design for a house in

From *Keramic Art of Japan* by G.A.Audsley and J.L.Bowes, published 1875

Berkeley Square in 1872, where it was repeated endlessly in various strutting and preening postures on a frieze, eighteen inches deep, along walls over twenty-five feet in length. Godwin encountered the peacock in the mural decorations by Henry Stacy Marks for Dromore Castle which Godwin had designed in partnership with Henry Crisp in 1867, and Godwin himself

over page
Thomas Jeckyll, dining room for F.R.Leyland at 49 Princes Gate (*Harmony in Blue and Gold: The Peacock Room*) as it was in 1890 (photo, National Monuments Record)
Decorations by Whistler, and his painting *Rose and Silver: La Princesse du Pays de la Porcelaine* (1864, now in the Freer Gallery) hanging above the mantelpiece. The Peacock Room was entirely dismantled in 1904 and is now reassembled (minus the china and Godwin furniture) in the Freer Gallery of Art, Washington DC.

James McNeill Whistler, The Peacock Room 1876–7
Courtesy of the Smithsonian Institution, Freer Gallery of Art, Washington DC. Detail of decoration on the south wall.

From *Keramic Art of Japan* by G.A.Audsley and J.L.Bowes, published 1875

designed a peacock wallpaper. A never-ending stream of precedents in the ten years before the Peacock Room could be cited, but more relevant is the continuous exposure of artists and designers to the peacock's common source—Japanese art.

Most forms of Japanese art were available by the early 1870s, for the South Kensington Museum acquired in 1871 and 1872 large collections of Oriental applied art and design. Exhibitions were held regularly, and the most important centre was Liverpool where in 1870 an Art Club was formed which had as its opening exhibition a display of Oriental art in a private house. This interest was largely generated by G.A.Audsley who produced a scholarly *catalogue raisonnée*, listing enamels, Persian, Chinese and Japanese ceramics as well as ivories, metals and lacquer work. These objects were mainly from the collection of the Japanese Consul James L. Bowes, who in 1875 published in co-operation with Audsley a luxuriously illustrated two-volume account of Japanese ceramics. Audsley and Bowes even reproduced the decorative motif used by Whistler in the Peacock Room and on his picture frames; and it seems very likely that Whistler became acquainted with their remarkable collection in the late sixties or early seventies when he often went to stay at Speke Hall near

Persian incense burner in the form of a peacock (one of a pair)
Brass and lapis lazuli, Coll. Mrs P.Hotchkis

Liverpool to paint, draw and etch portraits of the Leylands and their children. Probably more than an aesthetic coincidence too is the similarity between Whistler's haughty birds and the magnificent, proud Persian incense-burners owned by Alexander Ionides.

By the mid-seventies, the London public could actually obtain many examples of Japanese applied art. The most comprehensive collection of fans, kimonos and bric-à-brac could be found in Regent Street where Arthur Lasenby Liberty opened a shop in 1875, but well before this it was possible to buy various types of Oriental decoration. In 1871 Albert Moore's painting *Shuttlecock* was noted by the *Art Journal* critic for its colours 'which incline to tender and tertiary harmonies made known in this country by large importations of Japanese screens'. In 1872 the Oxford Street firm of Bontor and Collins was among the first to adapt Japanese materials to English work and a large number of folding screens were marketed, ornamented with coloured prints or Japanese silks and embroideries.

Whistler's screen, painted for F.R.Leyland, but which never reached him, dates from soon after this. Its asymmetrical arrangement of Church Tower and Thames bisected by a pier of Old Battersea Bridge is carried through—not unlike the Peacock Room—in a harmony of blue-green and gold. The sort of screens on sale in Oxford Street naturally did not evoke in London aesthetes quite the same associational response of nineteenth-century London with which Whistler surprised the public when the screen and his early Nocturnes were exhibited in the artist's first one-man exhibition in 1874. Whistler's own painted decoration is a Western artist's interpretation of a Japanese woodcut, which makes it unique. But by the end of the decade it was growing apparent that the Japanese craze could become the property of anyone; and in 1877 the *Art Journal* felt obliged to warn its readers of the increasing sale of bogus 'Japanese' goods which, by then, were flooding the market. By the 1880s, 'Art' could be bought for the price of a sunflower or a peacock's feather; and the style of painting which Whistler had established in fifteen years of serious aesthetic endeavour was being steadily undermined and identified with the whim of mere fashion.

Screen, with painted decoration by James McNeill Whistler 1872
Distemper (?) on brown paper, each panel 70 × 30 in. (177·8 × 76·2 cm)
Birnie Philip Bequest, University of Glasgow

3 'Art for Art's sake': Whistler versus Ruskin

Until the Grosvenor Gallery was opened in 1877, the Royal Academy remained the sole arbiter of public taste, and it was there that reputations were won or lost. In the 1870s it became apparent that the kind of painting and attitudes to art which Swinburne had forecast in 1868 were gradually, if slowly, infiltrating the rooms at Burlington House.

The Royal Academy exhibitions of the seventies presented a very mixed selection. Whistler stopped exhibiting there in 1872, but the work of Burne-Jones, Moore and Armstrong appeared regularly. Rossetti no longer showed his work in public but, of the Pre-Raphaelite generation, Arthur Hughes was typical of the sort of artist whose lyrical approach had always effortlessly coincided with the 'art for art's sake' style. Except for Holman Hunt, genuine Pre-Raphaelite realism had long since disappeared; and instead the buying public found a type of non-committal prettiness far more acceptable than aggressive symbolism.

Millais's painting continued to vary in quality as well as subject matter. He was at his best with the occasional landscape, but it was not long before he demonstrated a dangerous eclecticism for different painting techniques; and later became guilty of several tired pot-boilers which have nothing whatsoever to do with Pre-Raphaelitism. His subjects and titles lost their former clarity, and laid him open to criticism from progressive writers. In 1874, in a discussion on the charge of 'affectation' in Whistler's musical titles, even the conservative *Art Journal* found them more logical than Millais's. The anonymous critic cited Millais's *North West Passage* (which only depicted an old man explaining the North West Passage with the aid of a map to a little girl) as an example of a painting with a totally misleading title. William Powell Frith, the author of *Derby Day*, came in for criticism too with his offering of *Wandering Thoughts*. The reviewer's argument was that 'a picture should, before all things, be a beautiful scheme and design, both of lines and colour; and unless these qualities are secured, it is of very little significance what text the painter chooses to illustrate'. In the same year, Albert Moore's paintings received praise for exactly those qualities favoured by the *Art Journal*'s critic, and Moore's decorative intentions were at last fully recognized. Swinburne's aesthetic of an 'art for art's sake' had ultimately penetrated to the level of the Academy review, although in a considerably diluted form. But support like this was isolated, for the simple reason that the 'art for art's sake' painters always remained in a minority at the Academy and really independent artists, like Whistler, preferred to stage either one-man shows or exhibit in dealers' galleries. Furthermore, critical attention was inevitably distracted by artists like Edward Poynter, whose varied subject matter never failed to win the praise of Victorian critics, ever ready to admire size and be astonished at virtuosity.

Frederick Leighton's talents, like Poynter's, became similarly diversified over a wide range of themes and styles. Mythology, Eastern subjects, portraits and sculpture—as well as music—continued to increase the stature of the future President of the Royal Academy; and his house in Holland Park Road, built in 1866 by George Aitchinson, with its fairy-tale Arab Hall, a brilliant pastiche based on themes from Moorish Spain, became a social Mecca for its Olympian owner. Walter Crane planned a ceramic frieze in the Persian manner and William De Morgan contributed blue tiles to complete the polychromatic hot house interior, cooled by the lapping of water from a marble fountain.

As well as Leighton and a number of Grand Photographic Tradition followers, the 1870s also saw a new impetus in the category of social realism. Luke Fildes (1844–1927) attempted to do for painting what Dickens had done for literature. Works such as *The Return of a Penitent* (1874) were directly inspired by quotations from Dickens. Similarly, in 1874 Frank Holl (1845–88) exhibited a painting with the title *Deserted*, and in 1878, *Newgate: Committed for Trial* was shown at the Royal Academy. Both these artists, who left a deep lasting impression on Vincent Van Gogh when he lived in London, painted in a vigorously realistic style; and although the implications of their work had already been explored by writers, the strong social realism of their paintings appealed to an age which both witnessed the sad scenes depicted and thought it could do something to abolish them. It was against this varied and morally earnest background, in the year

in which the *Road to Ruin*—a series of five moral episodes in the style of Hogarth—was exhibited by Frith at the Royal Academy, that Whistler sued Ruskin for libel.

The basic facts of the trial are well known. Ruskin was appointed Slade Professor of Fine Art at Oxford in 1870, and since 1871 had been engaged in writing a series of letters, entitled *Fors Clavigera*, which were addressed to the working men of Britain, exhorting them to raise standards of production and to shun all that was imitation and sham by turning to Nature for instruction. It is true that these were admirable sentiments, but their application had been far more relevant to the state of craftsmanship thirty years before. It was quite clear that Ruskin was also out of touch with recent developments in design and painting, except perhaps for the work of Burne-Jones, in which he saw different qualities from those we might experience today. The sight of Whistler's *Nocturne in Black and Gold: the Falling Rocket*, exhibited alongside other paintings by him at the newly opened Grosvenor Gallery in 1877, was something that Ruskin had previously encountered; but to a philosophy which equated well-made art with moral stature, Whistler's Nocturnes were unacceptable. In *Fors Clavigera* for 2 July 1877, he therefore wrote:

> For Mr Whistler's own sake, no less than for the protection of the purchaser, Sir Coutts Lindsay ought not to have admitted works into the Gallery in which the ill-educated conceit of the artist so nearly approached the aspect of wilful imposture. I have seen, and heard, much of cockney impudence before now; but never expected to hear a coxcomb ask two hundred guineas for flinging a pot of paint in the public's face.

Remarks such as these, coming from the most influential art critic in England, were not likely to enhance a painter's reputation. Whistler considered that Ruskin had surpassed the bounds of fair comment, and, in consequence, sued him for libel.

George Aitchison, The Arab Hall, Leighton House, Holland Park Road, London 1877–9
(photo, Philip Mann)
Uppermost mosaic frieze designed by Walter Crane, 'Romanesque' capital heads carved by Randolph Caldecott.

James McNeill Whistler *Nocturne in Black and Gold: The Falling Rocket*
c. 1875
Oil on canvas 23¾ × 18⅜ in. (60·3 × 46·7 cm) Detroit Institute of Arts,
the Dexter M. Ferry Jr Fund
First exhibited at the Dudley Gallery in the winter exhibition 1875, and
then at the Grosvenor Gallery 1877.

Vincenzo Catena *Portrait of the Doge Andrea Gritti* (detail) 1523–31
Oil on canvas $38\frac{1}{4} \times 31\frac{1}{4}$ in. (97·2 × 79·4 cm) National Gallery, London

James McNeill Whistler *Nocturne in Blue and Gold: Old Battersea Bridge*
Oil on canvas 26¼ × 19¾ in. (66·7 × 50·2 cm) Tate Gallery, London
First exhibited at the Grosvenor Gallery 1877.

The head-on collision between Whistler and Ruskin centred in the trial on the concept of 'finish', ardently emphasized by all the witnesses for the defence; and Whistler's demands for artistic autonomy on the part of the modern painter. Whistler claimed that only a man 'whose life is passed in the practice of the science which he criticises' was justified in passing judgement on the work of others. Several of Whistler's paintings were brought into the courtroom, including *Nocturne in Blue and Gold: Old Battersea Bridge*, and the judge asked him 'is this part of the picture at the top Old Battersea Bridge?' 'Your Lordship is too close at present to the picture to perceive the effect which I intended to produce at a distance,' he replied. 'The spectator is supposed to be looking down the river towards London. . . . The thing is intended simply as a representation of moonlight. My whole scheme was only to bring about a certain harmony of colour.'

Frith was unable to see any worthwhile qualities in Whistler's work. Burne-Jones found *Nocturne in Blue and Gold: Old Battersea Bridge* 'bewildering in form' and showing 'no finish'—'it is simply a sketch'. To show what he meant by finish, Burne-Jones was asked to examine what was then believed to be a portrait by Titian of the Doge Andrea Gritti (see page 83). 'It shows finish,' he said. 'It is a very perfect sample of the highest finish of ancient art.' Later Albert Moore wrote a letter to the *Echo* explaining that the 'Titian' was an early one, 'and did not represent adequately the style and qualities which have obtained for him his great reputation.' Today, the painting is generally accepted as a work of Catena, but in 1878, as a Titian, it made Ruskin's defence even firmer.

The trial in fact never got off the ground, and, except for the support of William Michael Rossetti, the playwright William Gorman Wills and Albert Moore (whose paintings at Burlington House were always a bit of an embarrassment to the Academy, anyway) Whistler had no influential opinion to back his own: one or two painters who it seems had previously promised support, backed out at the last minute. The English legal system offered Whistler little opportunity of talking about aesthetics or painting techniques; for the trial was a battle of ideologies rather than real working methods. Whistler never went into detail

Old Battersea Bridge (photograph) *c.* 1877
National Monuments Record

about Japanese art. It would certainly not have meant much to Frith, although one might have expected better things from Burne-Jones, but his 'bewildering form' comment and the fact that his art was in debt to Ruskin's support (like that of so many successful Victorian painters), prevented any favourable concessions to Whistler's work. The reactions of Ruskin's witnesses showed that further argument was futile, but also revealed, in contrast, how far Whistler had progressed since his encounter with Rossetti and Swinburne; and how far he had extended his understanding of Japanese art by applying it to his paintings of the Thames.

There was really no excuse for ignorance of Japanese design principles, for certain types of Eastern art had become significant, not merely for their commercial manifestation in the Art Furniture of William Watt and others, but because of their analytical relevance to recent developments in the Western pictorial tradition. As well as Christopher Dresser (1834–1904), a practising designer who had actually visited Japan in 1877 and published a very thorough account of its architecture, art and art manufacturers, the writer who made one of the earliest efforts to bring together East and West was the American collector and art historian James Jackson Jarves (1818–87). In 1869 Jarves published the first of a series of articles on Japanese art, in which he expressed the firm belief that Western artists had something to learn from the Japanese. He explained how the Japanese artist *suggested* distances, perspectives and broad masses without stating them overtly as in Western art; that in the case of Western art 'we are given more to see, but we actually see less, because nothing is left to the imagination'. Jarves made the basic contrast between Japanese and Occidental compositional schema: 'It is common

Keisai Yeisen *Bridge over a River* before 1830
Yeisen was a pupil of Hokusai, and a member of the so-called 'Ukiyo-e' or 'Floating World' school.

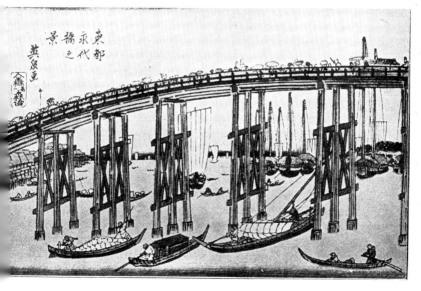

James McNeill Whistler *Nocturne in Blue and Silver: Cremorne Lights*
1872
Oil on canvas $19\frac{1}{2} \times 29\frac{1}{4}$ in. ($49 \cdot 5 \times 74 \cdot 3$ cm) Tate Gallery, London

On the left, a vestigial draped figure similar to those in the *Six Projects* (see plate pages 40–41) can be seen to emerge from a lower level of paint.

to omit foreground and background. Figures exist only in and by themselves, quite independent of local accessories. No attention is given to perspective, symmetry, light and shadow according to our rules. Japanese artists emphasize forcibly the main point, and neglect side issues or aids.'

A lot of Jarves's writing, in the further instalments of his research, show a William Morris-like concern for the state of the mass-produced product; but, unlike the European tradition of Morris's heritage, Jarves held up, instead, examples of Eastern manufacture. In fact, Christopher Dresser's own designs, remarkable for their simplicity and clean lines, precisely reflect Jarves's theories. Jarves was also capable of more sophisticated analyses, and in 1871 forcibly stated his preference for those colours which were translated from the 'musical harmonies' found in Japanese prints, in place of the meaningless and indiscriminate use of colour often found in Western art. This theory was beyond many artists in nineteenth-century England, but Whistler, for almost a decade, had been putting into practice exactly what Jarves advocated.

The outcome of the Whistler versus Ruskin trial—damages of one farthing to Whistler—brought a temporary lull in Whistler's fortunes and left him with a permanent grudge against society; but, in a broader context, the trial also made public a wide divergence of aesthetic opinion in nineteenth-century British art. The fashion for Art bric-à-brac, which by then was well underway, was easily identified with anyone, who, like Whistler, appeared to hold an extravagant aesthetic viewpoint. Whistler had already gathered a lot of publicity over the Peacock Room, but the trial brought even more. *Punch* cartoonists, such as Linley Sambourne, immediately cashed in, at a time when the general public had not even heard of Oscar Wilde. In many ways Whistler had been the scapegoat representing a silent minority, tired of Ruskin's dominance and indifference to contemporary art. Moreover, after the trial, Whistler was defended privately by several artists and in public by W.Macdonald, a 'grainer-marbler' from Manchester – one of the workmen for

Christopher Dresser, glass claret jug with silver mount, 1879–80
Victoria and Albert Museum, London

AN ARRANGEMENT IN "FIDDLE-DE-DEE."

Linley Sambourne 'An Arrangement in Fiddle-De-Dee'
From *Punch* October 6 1877

AN APPEAL TO THE LAW.

Linley Sambourne 'An Appeal to the Law' 1878
From *Punch* 7 December 1878
The caption reads: 'Naughty critic, to use bad language! Silly painter, to
go to Law about it!' The jury, represented in the form of Winsor &
Newton paint tubes, are given the words 'No Symphony with the
Defendant.'

whom Ruskin had written *Fors Clavigera*. By the 1880s the wheels
of reform begun by Ruskin over thirty years before had turned
full circle, and progressive artists were soon to look towards
France for new ideas and inspiration.

In the decade in which the trial took place, English artists, without crossing the Channel, had every opportunity of studying the
most progressive work of their French contemporaries. As a
result of the Franco-Prussian war, both Claude Monet and
Camille Pissarro came to stay in London for a short period; and
between 1870 and 1875 exhibitions of their work and that of

James McNeill Whistler *Arrangement in Grey: Self Portrait* 1872
Oil on canvas $29\frac{1}{2} \times 21$ in. $(74\cdot9 \times 53\cdot3$ cm) Detroit Institute of Arts,
bequest of Henry G. Stevens in memory of Ellen P. and Mary M. Stevens

Edouard Manet *La Femme au Perroquet c.* 1869
Oil on canvas $67\frac{3}{8} \times 50\frac{5}{8}$ in. $(171\cdot1 \times 128\cdot6$ cm) Metropolitan Museum
of Art, New York, gift of Erwin Davis 1889

their colleagues (who in 1874 in Paris became known as Impressionists) were held at the Bond Street Gallery of the French dealer Durand-Ruel. Degas, Manet, Monet, Pissarro, Renoir, Sisley, as well as Puvis de Chavannes, Fantin-Latour and Whistler were regular exhibitors. But the fact that Impressionist paintings could also be seen in London had little or no effect on English artists of that time, who were still dominated by the taste of the Academy; and the interest aroused was only enjoyed by the immediate Whistler circle. Some of the exhibitions were reviewed by the more progressive journals, and on one occasion, the *Athenaeum* astutely noticed that Manet and Whistler shared a considerable technical likeness. In 1872, Whistler's *Arrangement in Grey and Black No. II: A Portrait* (most likely to be the self-portrait now in Detroit) was hung with Manet's *Lady in Pink* (now known as *La Femme au Perroquet*); and it was said that both paintings were created 'out of the most unpromising materials, and to seize the eye and approach the mind by pictorial treatment'. But if some English critics could accept Whistler and Manet, they generally fought shy of Impressionism proper.

It was this liaison which brought Whistler once more into close contact with French painting (although it might be argued, with some justification, that throughout his life he never lost contact with it). In future years he was often referred to as an 'Impressionist' by English critics, a title which he objected to, but which to untutored English eyes was simply synonymous with 'modern'. For an initial period, though, the Thames did bring Whistler and Monet together: Monet's interpretation of the hazy river, painted during his stay in London in 1871, approximates to the structural ordering of similar themes by Whistler during the same period. In much the same way, Degas's refined, shimmering pastel studies of the Normandy coast in 1869 are immediately succeeded by the precise surface juxtaposition of river, horizon and sky, of Whistler's Nocturnes (see pages 88–89). But unlike Whistler, Degas and Monet never concentrated on night effects, and it was left to Whistler to make this particular genre his own.

If the 1870s witnessed, against a background of growing Art Industry, the development of Morris's design programme and

H.G.E.Degas *Marine* 1869
Pastel $13\frac{3}{8} \times 18\frac{1}{4}$ in. ($34 \times 46\cdot4$ cm) Cabinet des Dessins, Musée du Louvre, Paris

Whistler's demands for aesthetic independence, the early eighties saw both these viewpoints publicized in a very individual, if at times confused, way, by Oscar Wilde.

Oscar Wilde (1854–1900) came to live in London in 1879. At Oxford in 1878 he had won the Newdigate prize for poetry, and as an undergraduate was the most precociously aesthetic of his generation, indulging in the fashionable taste for blue and white china, Japanese art, the Pre-Raphaelites; and being generally impressed by everything and anyone connected with art. He was influenced by Ruskin as well as Walter Pater. Because of his charm and literary brilliance, Wilde was soon a part of London's artistic society. His major contribution to the Aesthetic Movement occurred in the United States, where he was sponsored by Richard D'Oyly Carte's American representative to give a series of lectures to coincide with the comic opera *Patience*, then playing in New York. Gilbert and Sullivan's *Patience* had first been produced by D'Oyly Carte (1844–1901) in London, at the Opéra Comique on 23 April 1881, and in October was moved to Carte's own recently built theatre, the Savoy. The opera was a satire on contemporary aestheticism, with its main comic character, Bunthorne, the fleshly poet, a compound of Whistler, Wilde and the easily caricatured aspects of Grosvenor Gallery taste. The fact that Wilde was the opera's publicist as well as its butt did not deter him from giving an account of what he regarded as the most promising aspects in English contemporary art and design. Under the title of *The English Renaissance of Art*, Wilde expounded his own version of the developments in literature and art from Keats up to his own day. Wilde's Renaissance really begins with the Pre-Raphaelites as purifiers in the field of painting and design; but it is clear from his interpretation of their activities, and his adulation of Ruskin's prose, that he was as much at home with the more mysterious aspects of Pre-Raphaelite painting as with the original ideas of the Brotherhood. To Wilde is owed the ultimate distinction of turning Pre-Raphaelitism into a *fin-de-siècle* movement. He made the lily another popular emblem (it had already been used as a traditional symbol of purity in the work of Rossetti). And with Morris-like simplicity he disarmingly justified the sunflower and lily as symbols of the Aesthetic Movement ('in spite of what Mr Gilbert may tell you'), because they were 'the two most perfect models of design, the most naturally adapted for decorative art— the gaudy leonine beauty of the one and the precious loveliness of the other, giving to the artist the most entire and perfect joy'.

In America, in addition to the *English Renaissance of Art*, Wilde gave a lecture on 'House Decoration', in which his debt to Morris and Whistler is very clear. That he should combine the ideas of Morris and Whistler in one narrative, first upholding the South Kensington Museum as the ideal place for the student of handicrafts and then the Peacock Room as an example of decorative purity, caused him no concern; but it doubtless became a secondary consideration in Whistler's ever-cooling friendship with him.

Wilde had met Whistler towards the end of 1881, and, in addition to sharing a number of aristocratic friends, they both lived, only doors apart, in Tite Street, Chelsea. The relationship

Linley Sambourne, 'Caricature of Oscar Wilde as a sunflower'
From *Punch* 25 June 1881

The caption reads: Aesthete of Aesthetes!
What's in a name?
The poet is WILDE
But his poetry's tame.

of their aesthetics has never been properly investigated; but it is obvious that, for the purposes of his American tour and a lecture he gave to the Royal Academy students in 1883, Wilde greatly benefited from his proximity to the painter. When, in 1890, Whistler accused Wilde of plagiarism and broke off relations with him for good, he referred to him as 'my St John', which suggests the possibility that at one time he had cherished the notion that, in America, Wilde might act more as a publicity agent for Whistler's paintings than for D'Oyly Carte's opera. This would partly explain why, as Whistler admitted, he 'crammed' the poet with so many of his own ideas. For a time Whistler enjoyed Wilde's company and the publicity that ensued, but as Wilde's reputation as a literary figure and wit grew, so his friendship with the painter dwindled. It was considerably lowered in temperature by Wilde's writing a not altogether favourable review of Whistler's 'Ten O'Clock' lecture in 1885. As with Ruskin before, but this time with greater justification, Whistler objected to the criticism of someone who was not a practising artist, and who, in this case, had only half digested his ideas.

The publicity which Wilde gave to the Aesthetic Movement was only equalled by *Punch*'s satire on it. From 1878 *Punch*'s cartoonist, George du Maurier (1834–96), regularly poked Philistine fun at the Movement, with his aesthetic family, the Cimabue Browns, the painter Maudle, and the poet Postlethwaite. Du Maurier had known Whistler in Paris in the 1850s, when he had tried, unsuccessfully, to become a painter. His ambitions were partly frustrated by the loss of sight in one eye; but by the sixties he had established himself as a versatile illustrator in a decade which produced a vigorous revival in the graphic arts. In London he was on the fringe of the Whistler set but never a real part of it, and he remained a commentator rather than a practitioner in aesthetic matters.

In the early 1880s, Whistler was the source of a great deal of Aesthetic public confusion, in America as well as in England, as D'Oyly Carte's opera *Patience* had shown. Aestheticism, as opposed to Philistinism, had almost become part of tradition; and the public, at first expecting to scorn the antics of the Aesthetes, was soon won over by *Patience*'s superficial artistry, with its Liberty costumes and extravagant sentiments. To add to the muddle of an Aesthete's personal identity, Wilde, with his references to Keats, the art of Greece and Japan, Morris and Whistler, must, at times, have left in his listeners' minds little more than a confused blur.

In 1878 Whistler had challenged the English art world to accept his offer of enjoying the aesthetic sensation of a particularly original form of art. It had not been accepted. When, in 1885, the guarantee of acceptable modernity was the ownership of Art Furniture, peacock feathers, William Morris wallpaper and listening to Oscar Wilde, it was time for Whistler to make another stand. The result was the 'Ten O'Clock' lecture, given in the Princes Hall on 20 February 1885. In it Whistler attempted to disassociate himself from the Aesthetic Movement: 'Yes, Art—that has of late become . . . a sort of common topic for the tea table. Art is upon the Town!—to be chucked under the chin by the passing gallant—to be enticed within the gates of the householder—to be coaxed into company, as a proof of culture and refinement.' The lecture was directed too against all 'false prophets', i.e. Ruskin: 'Then the Preacher appointed . . . Sage of the Universities'; and Morris's Arts and Crafts Movement received several well directed barbs: 'That, could we but change our habits and climate . . . we should again require the spoon of Queen Anne, and pick at our peas with the fork of two prongs . . . And so, for the flock, little hamlets grow near Hammersmith, and the steam horse is scorned.' But, it was Oscar Wilde's ideas on dress reform and the aesthetic climate for which he was responsible, that Whistler ridiculed most of all. The alternative offered by Whistler in exchange for all this (apart, of course, from his own painting) was a new attitude to art rather than a fresh interpretation of art's place in society. He denied that an 'artistic period' had ever existed, only Art, which had survived throughout the centuries, regardless of transient fashion, social or economic considerations. Therefore Art could never be affected for the worse by would-be reformers, moralizers or aesthetes. With a certain lucid perversity, at times reminiscent of Wilde's own rhetoric, Whistler removed from the layman's shoulders all responsibility and care for Art's future.

Besides these strictures, and stripped of its Old Testament trimmings, the 'Ten O'Clock' lecture is full of a sound painter's

George Du Maurier 'Modern Aesthetics'
From *Punch* 14 December 1877

sense. Against the background of Victorian narrative painting, Whistler showed that Art was an extension neither of literature nor morality. Terms associated with ordinary visual experience and used in writing—lofty, vast, infinite—had no place in the artist's vocabulary. To counteract Ruskin's insistence on 'truth to nature', Whistler emphasized instead that Art never directly copied Nature, and that Nature's real significance lay elsewhere: 'But the artist is born to pick, and choose, and group with science, these elements, that the result may be beautiful—as the musician gathers his notes, and forms his chords, until he bring forth from chaos glorious harmony. To say to the painter, that Nature is to be taken as She is, is to say to the player, that he may sit on the piano.'

If in the lecture Whistler refused to capitulate to the Aesthetic Movement *per se*, he naturally implied that he regarded himself as the only modern exponent of a tradition which he went to some trouble to describe. His art history lesson is of gigantic

Albert Moore, studies for *Battledore* and *Shuttlecock* c. 1871
14 × 9$\frac{3}{16}$ in. (35·5 × 23·3 cm) Ashmolean Museum, Oxford

Helena in Troas, set and costume designs by E.W. Godwin, Hengler's Cirque, 1886 (photo, Victoria and Albert Museum)

One of Helena's handmaidens is Constance (Mrs Oscar) Wilde.

James McNeill Whistler *Parasol for Lady Archibald Campbell* 1881/5
Pencil and watercolour $11\frac{1}{2} \times 9\frac{1}{4}$ in. (29·2 × 23·3 cm) Birnie Philip
Bequest, University of Glasgow

James McNeill Whistler *Design for a Garden Trellis* for the Campbells'
country house, Coombe, Surrey 1881
Pen, pencil and wash 7 × 10 in. (17·7 × 25·3 cm) Birnie Philip Bequest,
University of Glasgow

The note in Whistler's hand reads: 'The trellis work must in the arrangement be pale primrose colour—anything at all of an orange tendency
would make the whole hot—the doors and roofing will give the orange.'

significance for nineteenth-century painting; and in it he incor-
porated not only his aesthetic views, but the basic ingredients of
his own stylistic development: Velasquez, Greek, and Japanese art.

On rare occasions Whistler did design personal items for his
friends which might be described as Aesthetic Movement
objects. But the distinction is that such commissions, in contrast with Morris's wallpaper or mass-produced Art Industry,
were of an essentially private nature and never repeated. They
all reveal unmistakable economy of means, and were usually
accompanied by Whistler's butterfly signature. The work which
he did for Lady Archibald Campbell was in this sort of spirit.

Scene from *As you Like It* (photograph)
Birnie Philip Bequest, University of Glasgow
Lady Archibald Campbell as Orlando in the grounds at Coombe, 1884.

James McNeill Whistler *Note in Green and Brown: Orlando at Coombe*
(Lady Archibald Campbell) 1884
$5\frac{7}{8} \times 3\frac{1}{2}$ in. (14·9 × 8·9 cm) Birnie Philip Bequest, University of Glasgow

Besides painting her portrait as *Arrangement in Black: Lady in the Yellow Buskin*, and planning a garden trellis for the Campbells' country house, Whistler designed her a parasol in pale green silk. The Campbells' Surrey home, Coombe, was also a centre for amateur dramatics. In 1885 the Campbells started a company called the *Pastoral Players* which came mostly under the artistic direction of E.W.Godwin. At Coombe the previous year Godwin had produced *As You Like It*, in the open air. Lady Campbell herself played Orlando; and Whistler depicted her on a tiny panel, dressed in black, against the leaf-green background of Coombe's parkland. Godwin had always been interested in the theatre, and was brought into professional contact with it through his relationship with Ellen Terry (1847–1928) who was then

'The Hanging Committee of the Liverpool Art Society' 1891 (photograph). The group includes Whistler (*extreme left*).
Birnie Philip Bequest, University of Glasgow

separated from her elderly husband, G.F. Watts. Godwin's liaison with her lasted until 1875; and a year later he married Beatrix Philip who, after Godwin's death, became Mrs Whistler in 1888. For Ellen Terry, Godwin designed a costume 'like almond blossom' when she appeared as Portia in the Bancrofts' production of the *Merchant of Venice* at the Prince of Wales Theatre in 1875. He was also responsible for the settings, radical for nineteenth-century British theatre because of their elegance and archaeological accuracy. It was not so much these sets, but the stark simplicity of his last production *Helena in Troas* (Henglers 1886) that directly inaugurates the revolution in modern theatre design begun by Godwin's talented son Edward Gordon Craig, born to Ellen Terry in 1872.

Except for some of the artists who became members of the

James McNeill Whistler *Interior of the British Artists Exhibition* 1887
Pen $7\frac{7}{8} \times 6\frac{1}{4}$ in. ($20 \times 15 \cdot 9$ cm) Ashmolean Museum, Oxford

James McNeill Whistler *Colour scheme for the dining room at Aubrey House*
1872–3
Body colour on brown paper $7\frac{1}{4} \times 5$ in. (18·4 × 12·7 cm) Birnie Philip
Bequest, University of Glasgow

New English Art Club in 1886, and those already converted, the 'Ten O'Clock' philosophy fell on deaf ears when it was first given. But in the eighties gradual changes did take place in the exhibition of paintings which in part reflect Whistler's growing influence on English art. With the opening of the Grosvenor Gallery in 1877, Sir Coutts Lindsay had already provided an opportunity for progressive artists who either did not wish, or were unable to have their work hung at the Royal Academy. Exhibition was by invitation; and some care was taken over the hanging, so that the paintings were better spaced than on the overcrowded walls of the Academy. But the conditions were by no means ideal; and the overall effect was spoilt by a faded red damask wallpaper. Generally though, exhibiting conditions in English galleries were far worse. Pictures were hung like postage stamps, often without an inch of wall to separate them; and lighting was poor. This was the situation at the run-down Society of British Artists before Whistler was elected President in 1887. The innovations which he brought to the Society—including the paintings of Claude Monet—were far too radical for its members: Whistler was obliged to resign after two years. However, in a short space of time, the number of paintings on the walls was reduced and the viewing conditions greatly improved by a system of diffused lighting, introduced by means of a velarium suspended from the ceiling—a device which he patented.

The exhibiting arrangements Whistler made for the Royal Society of British Artists were never taken as far as those for his own exhibitions; or for the colour schemes prepared for Aubrey House, the home of his patron, W.C.Alexander. For the dining room at Aubrey House, in 1872 or 1873, several years before the dado was emphasized in the fashionable interior, Whistler planned to divide the wall space with zones of pale blue and yellow that bears closer comparison with a 1950 painting by Mark Rothko than with the fruit-filled borders of an Aesthetic Movement wallpaper. Naturally in the nineteenth century the full aesthetic implications of such schemes could never be realized in terms of a finished work of art; and it was left to artists and designers of a younger generation than Whistler's to carry these prophetic achievements into the twentieth century.

4 Aesthetic arts and crafts to Art Nouveau

'And now has set in a fashion, dedicated to her most sacred Majesty, Queen Anne, a fashion which has developed much of really good character, and which, after all, properly applied, is really bringing us back to old English work . . . It is but fair to say to Messrs Street, RA, Norman Shaw, RA, Waterhouse, ARA, E.W.Godwin, W.Burges, P.Webb, and other architects, and to Messrs Morris and Co., Messrs Crace, Messrs Gillow, Messrs Jackson and Graham, Messrs Jeffery, and other well-known firms, much praise is due for their efforts in the cause of artistic design.'

Sir Robert Edis is only one of many writers to take a broad view of the art of his own age, massing together under the umbrella of 'Queen Anne' so many plainly contrasting trends in style. Whether Greek or Japanese, medieval or clearly modern, any designer or firm that successfully married art with industry and revealed the slightest spark of originality or missionary zeal for making a positive impression on contemporary taste was admitted to the Aesthetic Movement's hall of fame.

It might be argued that if Whistler, as a serious fine artist, objected to being associated with the Aesthetic Movement, William Morris as the designer with a social conscience would object to being linked with firms whose methods of production were different from his own. So far as we know Morris never made a positive stand on this issue. But it was through writers like Edis—and many more besides—that Morris's influence as the initiator of the Arts and Crafts Movement became inevitably linked with the Art Industry of the Aesthetic Movement. It is ironic that Morris, instead of helping to bring art to the masses, unwittingly contributed to art's exclusiveness. The fulfilment of his relentless maxim, 'What business have we with art at all, unless all can share it', was frustrated by his total abhorrence, on social as well as aesthetic grounds, of the machine as an acceptable means of production. Many of his designs were costly to manufacture, and therefore only available to the audience for whom Edis had written his book: the middle and upper classes. As a luxury product, Morris's work was unfortunately not within the scope of the lower strata of Victorian society. But to those Victorians who could afford to employ him, and who prided themselves on combining reform with innovation, an Aesthetic Movement with a social conscience proved an agreeable indulgence. This conflict between theory and practice sets Morris apart from designers such as Henry Cole, who attempted to combine 'art' with industry as early as 1847 when the firm of Summerly's Art Manufacturers was founded; or Christopher Dresser who included the machine as an integral part of his design programme.

The simplicity and purity of craftsmanship which Morris strove for was based on his admiration for Pre-Raphaelite idealism in the 1850s whereas Sir Robert Edis's ideas were borne on the wave of enthusiasm for the Aesthetic Movement. But it is just as impossible to overlook Edis as it is to neglect *Patience* or Oscar Wilde when considering the atmosphere in which the Arts and Crafts Movement blossomed in the eighties. For this same decade produced designers who not only shared Morris's admiration for the art of the past but who were also responsible for the first glimmerings of Art Nouveau, a movement that was to sweep Europe in the last years of the nineteenth century.

Arthur Heygate Mackmurdo (1851–1942) more than anyone else combined both these Janus-like tendencies in one design: the title-page for his book on *Wren's City Churches* (1883). The Society for the Protection of Ancient Buildings had been formed by Morris in 1877; so it is clear that the function of Mackmurdo's book—a plea for the preservation of Wren's architecture—was conceived in the Morris tradition. At the same time, Mackmurdo employed a decorative form which violently exaggerated the sedate regularity of any Morris design it might resemble. Yet the spirit of this work was still a product of Morris's reform movement seen in the context of the Aesthetic Movement, rather than a deliberate attempt at *fin-de-siècle* Art Nouveau which it innocently predates. In other words, to accuse Mackmurdo of ignoring Ruskin or not looking carefully at nature would be wrong. At the same time Mackmurdo's individuality is quite

WREN'S CITY CHURCHES

BY
A·H·MACKMURDO, A·R·I·B·A,
1883
G. ALLEN, SUNNYSIDE, ORPINGTON, KENT.

obvious; and his interpretation of plant forms places him closer to Burne-Jones than to the original Pre-Raphaelite view of truth to nature.

Although the pioneering spirit of Morris was behind the activities of the Century Guild, and Morris's designs were admired, his social strictures were found irksome. Reservations on these lines appeared in the preface to the Century Guild's magazine, the *Hobby Horse*, which first appeared in 1884:

'As an art craftsman he is our master; but we hesitate to follow him in his endeavour to agitate for state intervention as a possible panacea of poverty; or to accept his belief in parliament as apportioner of poverty. Poverty, injustice and crime are to us the natural result of class character, and class character like individual character acts automatically according to its bulk of higher human elements: which bulk cannot be increased artificially.'

These are traditional Victorian sentiments but they did not prevent the work of the Century Guild from following the Morris pattern reasonably closely, for in addition to the products of their workshops, the members of the Century Guild made a determined effort to redefine contemporary art and its function in society. They attempted to rescue the missionary spirit of the Aesthetic Movement by permanently restoring what *Patience*'s satire had tried to destroy. In this respect Selwyn Image was particularly resourceful, as he saw a higher purpose behind art than had been preached by the confused popularizers of the Aesthetic Movement. In his lectures Image was anxious to establish himself and his colleagues on a more elevated plane: 'The sphere of Art is in the region of the imagination, and the office of the imagination is to render us sensitive to the experience of some of the most exquisite pleasures of which our nature is capable' (1884). Image's ideas on art—a fusion of Ruskin and Baudelaire—are characteristic of several artists and critics who drew inspiration

A.H.Mackmurdo, title page to *Wren's City Churches*, published 1883
$9\frac{1}{4} \times 7$ in. $(23 \cdot 5 \times 17 \cdot 8$ cm) printed by G.Allen, Orpington, Kent

A.H.Mackmurdo *Thorns and Butterflies c.* 1884
Printed cotton, possibly made by Simpson and Godlee, Manchester
William Morris Gallery, Walthamstow (photo, J.W.Mellish)

Arthur Burgess 'Plant Forms'
From Ruskin's obituary of Burgess in the *Hobby Horse* 1887
(Burgess drew and engraved the illustrations for Ruskin's books.)

over page
Century Guild Inventions Exhibition
From the *Hobby Horse* 1887
Furniture and fabric designs by Mackmurdo and other members of the
Century Guild in the show rooms of Wilkinson & Son, 8 Old Bond
Street.

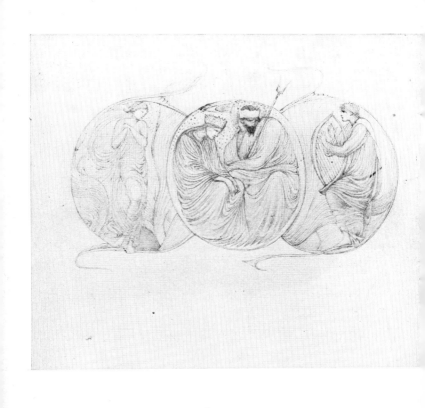

Edward Burne-Jones, study for *The Story of Orpheus* 1875
Pencil 9 × 12 in. (22·9 × 30·5 cm) Tate Gallery, London

from the more serious implications of Aesthetic Movement theory.

This framework provided the theoretical background to the work of C.F.A.Voysey (1857–1941), although the simplicity and sheer architectural practicality of his mature work were to transcend Image's high-flown moral purpose. Familiarity with the wallpapers and printed textiles of the Century Guild, rather than collective theories, influenced Voysey in his early career; and eventually placed him, in spite of his objections, firmly in the decade of Art Nouveau.

Later, the same reluctance on Voysey's part to have his work associated with Art Nouveau led to his objection to being categorized as an important precursor of twentieth-century architecture. Looking back on his achievements, Voysey's reactions to both these interpretations of his work can be justified by his own undeniable originality. In architecture and fabric designs Mackmurdo's influence is self-evident, but there is an individual clarity about Voysey's two-dimensional patterns making them difficult to catalogue stylistically. Whereas we can understand the formal relationship between Mackmurdo's designs and the proto-Art Nouveau paintings of Burne-Jones, we hesitate in the case of Voysey to take such an easy way out. Gone are the measured cadences of Morris's repeats. Instead, Voysey's wallpapers and chintzes, whether of the eighties or the nineties, all have their own organic logic which determines the size and rhythm of the repeated pattern. Forms are simpler than Mackmurdo's; and all the patterns respect the implicit flatness of the ground, by denying space and making little concession to the usual conventions of depth.

Voysey's equivocal reluctance to have his work associated with Art Nouveau (he wrote in 1904, 'I think the condition which has made *Art Nouveau* possible is a distinctly healthy development, but at the same time the manifestation of it distinctly unhealthy and revolting') reveals his support for reform but a lack of sympathy with the *fin-de-siècle* spirit. The fact that his architecture can now be seen, not just as a development of the domestic revival work of the Aesthetic Movement, but as a forerunner of a lot of modern architecture as well, only adds to his stature.

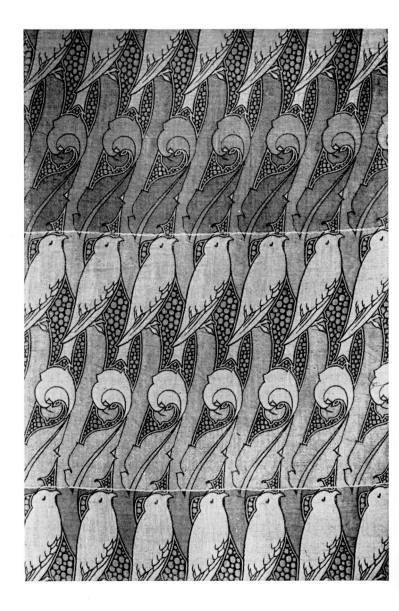

124

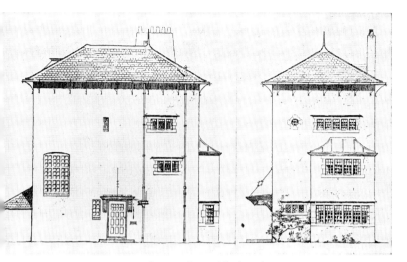

C.F.A.Voysey, No. 12 The Parade, Bedford Park *c*. 1891
Line drawing by courtesy of John Brandon-Jones

C.F.A.Voysey, Sample strip, reversible double-cloth, *c*. 1897
Silk and wool, woven by Alexander Morton & Co. 105 × 46 in.
(266·7 × 116·8 cm) Whitworth Art Gallery, University of Manchester
(Compare with plate on page 118)

Mackmurdo's influence was not confined to his architecture
and fabric designs, but included his illustrated books. The *Hobby
Horse* had been started in 1884 by Horne and Mackmurdo and,
after changing to a larger format in 1886, was to run till 1892.
Selwyn Image had provided a design for the cover which reappeared on every issue. The *Hobby Horse* was the first periodical
to create a serious interest in the medium of book production,
which meant treating the printed page as a well-considered
unity. As well as being the first of a whole series of illustrated
periodicals in the eighties and nineties, both Continental and

British, the *Hobby Horse* can also be seen in the context of a steady development of new attitudes to the graphic arts which by the end of the century resulted in an entirely new status for illustration.

The resurgence and quality of the graphic arts in the 1860s, like so many reform movements in nineteenth-century British art, is directly related to previous achievements of the Pre-Raphaelites. Moxon's illustrated edition of *Tennyson* appeared in 1857, containing wood engravings after original drawings by Rossetti, Holman Hunt and Millais. Although no effort was made to produce a volume that integrated text with illustrations in the style of the eighties and nineties, Moxon's *Tennyson* did provide an opportunity for the Pre-Raphaelites' originality to reach a wider audience. Rossetti's contributions were very similar to the compositions of his watercolours in the fifties; but Hunt's illustration, *The Lady of Shalott*, with its swirling lines and feeling of claustrophobic imprisonment, makes a direct approach to the age of Beardsley and the graphic art of the nineties.

In the sixties, for periodicals like *Once a Week*, Millais, Charles Keene, Frederick Walker, Frederick Sandys and Arthur Hughes all proved themselves capable of broadening the dimensions of what had previously been regarded as mere illustration. They showed that it was possible to combine tonal richness with dramatic characterization in a way which had never been attempted before. It was in this decade that Du Maurier established the basis for future recognition with drawings for the *Cornhill Magazine*, *Good Words*, and occasionally *Punch*. Du Maurier's parodies of Pre-Raphaelite sentiments for *Punch* in 1866 foreshadow by more than a decade his similar comments as *Punch*'s resident satirist of the Aesthetic Movement.

Selwyn Image, title page of the *Hobby Horse* 1890
Engraving 9 × 6¾ in. (22·9 × 17·1 cm)

THE CENTURY GUILD

HOBBY HORSE

LONDON: PUBLISHED BY
THE PROPRIETORS AT
THE CHISWICK PRESS.

THE LADY OF SHALOTT.

PART I.

I.

On either side the river lie
Long fields of barley and of rye,
That clothe the wold and meet the sky;
And thro' the field the road runs by
      To many-tower'd Camelot;

George Du Maurier *A Legend of Camelot—Part 3* 17 March 1866
Du Maurier's satire appeared in *Punch* in five weekly instalments.

William Holman Hunt *The Lady of Shalott* 1857
Engraving $3\frac{5}{8} \times 3\frac{7}{8}$ in. ($9\cdot2 \times 9\cdot8$ cm)

Eagerly following the achievements of the sixties was Walter Crane (1845–1915). Born in Liverpool, Crane lived in London from the age of twelve. Years later he remembered the impact which Ruskin's *Modern Painters* and Pre-Raphaelitism had made on him—or at least it was Millais's *A Dream of the Past: Sir Isumbras at the Ford* which he especially recalled. Through Ruskin's influence he became an apprentice at the office of the wood-engraver William James Linton; and during the sixties he was

For me, for me, for me!
And it was deeply
laden
With good things
for me!

naturally attracted to the work of Rossetti, Hunt and Millais. It was not until 1865 that Crane started working on the toy-books which were to make him famous in the seventies and eighties. The very early ones, *Cock Robin* and *Dame Trot and her Comical Cat* (1865–6), were published by Warne and Co., and Crane later remembered that he was specifically requested not to make his children 'unnecessarily covered with hair . . . long hair at that time being considered a dangerous innovation of Pre-Raphaelite tendency'.

It was largely due to his association with the colour printer Edmund Evans, who skilfully transferred Crane's original drawings to the printed page, that the success of the sixpenny and shilling toy-books was ensured. This partnership combined with Crane's discovery of Japanese prints in the mid-sixties helped him establish a mature style. As with so many other artists in France and England the decorative possibilities offered by Japanese art proved a decisive influence. Crane described this himself: 'Black was used as a colour as well as for outlines, hatching disappeared, and tints as harmonious as possible, within the somewhat crude and limited range of printing ink, were sought after.' *The Fairy Ship*, published by Routledge in 1869, is a good example of the early influence of Japanese prints on Crane's work. The flat planes of simple colour and the daring asymmetrical arrangement were to be fully exploited in future years.

Crane's was a many-sided personality. In addition to creating interior schemes such as the one for the Ionides, and designing the toy-books, he was also a very active socialist. He joined the Socialist League in 1883, and became the first President of the Art Workers' Guild in 1884. This was followed by his Presidency, between 1888 and 1890, of the Arts and Crafts Exhibition Society. Crane also designed wallpapers, manufactured by Messrs Jeffrey, and ceramics manufactured by Maw and Co. and by Pilkingtons. In addition to writing several books on design

Walter Crane from *The Fairy Ship* 1869
Engraved and printed in colour by Edmund Evans 8 × 6¼ in. (20·3 × 15·9 cm) published by George Routledge Ltd

theory and socialism he was a regular exhibitor at the Grosvenor Gallery, although his paintings show a frigid classicism—which was one of the less successful consequences of familiarity with Italian painting. Crane is chiefly remembered today for his toy-books; but his prolific versatility is a further illustration of how late-nineteenth-century Britain could accept a socialist who was capable of working for aristocrats as well as ideals.

The toy-books of the Aesthetic Movement, especially Crane's, were produced in their thousands; so their appeal was, under-standably, not limited to Britain. Apart from Crane's painting which could be seen abroad (he regularly exhibited at the Paris Salon) it was mainly his graphic work that appealed to the French. Often the naïve sentiments of the toy-books were modi-fied to provide greater appeal for adults. This was the case with *Flora's Feast* (Cassell 1888), in which the symbolic language given to flowers was a source of *fin-de-siècle* admiration for the French poet Comte Robert de Montesquiou who compared Crane's dream creations to the flower maidens of Wagner's *Parsifal* in his poem 'Chef des Odeurs Suaves'.

The bold colours of Crane's work were often modified by other illustrators of the Aesthetic Movement; but many of them, like Crane, had Edmund Evans to thank for furthering their careers. In fact it was Evans's technical advances in the field of engraving and coloured book illustration that produced such a variety of effects in the work of Kate Greenaway and Randolph Caldecott.

Kate Greenaway (1846–1901) was the daughter of John Greena-way, a prominent wood-engraver and draughtsman who was an early contributor to the *Illustrated London News* and *Punch*; and it was through her father, a friend of Edmund Evans, that she began her career. Her soft pastel hues, faithfully translated by Evans, are the female counterparts to Walter Crane's boyish style. With her drawing she created an entirely new world of delicately-poised nursery figures inhabiting a never-never

Walter Crane from *Flora's Feast* 1888
Engraved and printed in colour by Edmund Evans $9\frac{3}{4} \times 7\frac{1}{4}$ in. (24·8 × 18·4 cm) published by Cassell & Co. From the library of Glasgow School of Art

he fond Convolvulus still clings,
The Honeysuckle spreads his
wings.

Tom, Tom, the piper's son,
He learnt to play when he was young,
He with his pipe made such a noise,
That he pleased all the girls and boys.

Randolph Caldecott from *John Gilpin* 1878
Engraved and printed in colour by Edmund Evans 8 × 14¾ in. (20·3 × 37·5 cm) published by Frederick Warne & Co. From the library of Glasgow School of Art

◀ Kate Greenaway from *Mother Goose* or *The Old Nursery Rhymes* 1885
Engraved and printed in colour by Edmund Evans 4½ × 2¾ in. (11·4 × 7 cm) first published by George Routledge Ltd 1885 in English, German and French, in an edition of 66,000. From the library of Glasgow School of Art

countryside of arcadian purity far from the big city smoke. These agreeable and edifying sentiments enjoyed widespread appeal, and went far in defining the taste of the Aesthetic Movement. Today Kate Greenaway's style appears essentially escapist; but in her own lifetime a loyal translation of nature's purity, maintained by a long admiration for Ruskin, easily insured her lasting popularity.

A tougher, more masculine approach to the illustration of children's books was provided by Randolph Caldecott (1846–86). Caldecott's comparatively short working life in this medium

over page
Paul Gauguin *Breton Peasant Women* 1886 28¼ × 35¾ in. (72 × 91 cm) Bayrische Staatsgemaldessammlungen, Munich

was confined to about eight years; and he too took advantage of the skills of Edmund Evans, who produced his first toy-books in 1878. Caldecott used a number of different styles, ranging from the purely descriptive to the rollicking humour of books like *John Gilpin* (Warne 1878) and the *Great Panjandrum Himself* (Routledge 1885) which have a sense of the ridiculous clearly inherited from Rowlandson. Caldecott often included in his plates the red-brick houses and milk-maid costumes loosely

Paul Gauguin *Breton Girl* 1886
Chalk 18⅝ × 12½ in. (47·9 × 31·8 cm) Burrell Collection, City of Glasgow Art Gallery and Museum
A study for *Breton Peasant Women* (page 136).

identified as 'Queen Anne'; and his illustrations were usually conceived in broad flat areas of colour which invited many imitators towards the end of the century. What really distinguished Caldecott's work from Kate Greenaway's and Walter Crane's was his wiry line and vivid characterization. His illustrations are remarkable for their implication of swift movement which is never emphasized at the expense of surface decoration.

It was this apparently simple but daring draughtsmanship

Randolph Caldecott from *Breton Folk* 1880
$4\frac{3}{4} \times 3\frac{1}{2}$ in. ($12\cdot1 \times 8\cdot9$ cm)

which appealed so much to Gauguin, who owned one of Caldecott's coloured books in Brittany in 1886, and is recorded as extravagantly praising Caldecott's way of drawing geese. Curiously enough, Caldecott was no stranger to Brittany either, and illustrated a record of his observations of Breton folklore in a book called *Breton Folk, An Artistic Tour in Brittany*, published in 1880 with a text by Henry Blackburn. It is intriguing too that one of the best summaries of Caldecott's life appeared as an obituary notice by the English critic Claude Phillips in the *Gazette des Beaux Arts* in 1886. The novelist J.K.Huysmans was also an admirer of Caldecott's art, and mentioned him, along with Greenaway and Crane, in his *Salon Review* for 1881. It seems likely that, to the French, Caldecott pictured the vivid nostalgic images of old England which Des Esseintes was so eager to experience as the hero of Huysmans's *fin-de-siècle* novel *A Rebours* (1884). Indeed, this *fin-de-siècle* admiration for the elegance of eighteenth-century life, given added impetus by the De Goncourts, makes Gauguin's enthusiasm for Caldecott more understandable in the decade of Symbolism.

Such an interpretation of Caldecott's work was of course quite unacceptable to the English, for whom Caldecott remained the innocent entertainer of well-bred children. But the work of a number of English artists faced a different critical reception in France in the later years of the century. Burne-Jones was a case in point, for his paintings and designs were shown regularly in Paris from 1884 to 1893; and it is easy to see why the mysterious content of his art appealed to the Symbolist generation.

It was probably Whistler, more than any other artist, whose articulate system of aesthetics directly appealed to the Symbolists. The misty ambiguity of his paintings and a philosophy that was reluctant to accept nature at face value was easily interpreted in Paris as anti-Realist. Whistler's ideas became more widely known in 1888, when the 'Ten O'Clock' lecture was translated into French by Stéphane Mallarmé, who had been introduced to Whistler by Monet. The fact that the aesthetic impressionism of Whistler's prose was translated by so influential a figure as Mallarmé increased Whistler's reputation in France, and coincided with the Symbolists' desire to escape the French Realist tradition consolidated by Zola and the Impressionists.

Edward Burne-Jones *The Heart of the Lotus* 1880
Design for a fabric, present whereabouts unknown

Apart from the 'English Symbolists', many artists took the opportunity of combining traditional forms with aesthetic awareness. This sort of art often goes under the title 'High Victorian', and is typified by the St Johns Wood School which shows Victorian society preening itself in exotic surroundings, blissfully unaware of the collapse of social mores that was to come in the mid-nineties. It is true that Sir Lawrence Alma-Tadema (1836–1912) had been painting themes from Roman life since the sixties, and really shares a niche with Albert Moore and others in that decade; but he takes on greater significance later, not only as a social reporter in disguise but also as an artist who, conventionally aloof from sunflowers and lilies, nevertheless absorbed some of the pictorial elegance so typical of the Aesthetic Movement. Today he is best remembered for his classical genre scenes rather than for his interpretation of Maeterlinck's *Pelléas and Mélisande*; but a more critical look at some of his pictures and a closer examination of his use of paint will reveal that he can, occasionally, achieve a brilliance of effect and delicacy of arrangement which has for too long been masquerading in Roman fancy dress.

There were several artists who with Alma-Tadema might be regarded as 'second string' Aesthetes. They too refused to flaunt the lily or the sunflower in a way that might be construed as provocative. As might be expected, compromises such as these usually betrayed an affiliation either to the Burne-Jones type or to Leighton's allegorical portraits. Charles Edward Perugini (1839–1919), like Leighton, bridged the gap between portraiture and allegory, thereby avoiding commitment to a photographic likeness. By calling one of his works *Peonies*, Perugini continued a tradition established by Albert Moore who named his paintings by referring to a single blossom or fruit, thus giving the key and mood to the whole. This was probably the source for some of the theories connected with the aesthetic symbolism of the Ricketts and Shannon circle in the nineties. Charles Ricketts (1866–1931)

Sir Lawrence Alma-Tadema *A Foregone Conclusion* 1885
Oil on canvas $12\frac{1}{4} \times 9$ in. (31·1 × 22·9 cm) Tate Gallery, London

THE FISHER-
-MAN AND
HIS SOVL

TO H.S.H
ALICE, PRINCESS
OF MONACO.

EVERY evening
the young Fisherman
went out upon the
sea, and threw his
nets into the water.
When the wind
blew from the land he caught nothing, or but
little at best, for it was a bitter and black-
winged wind, and rough
waves rose up to meet it.
But when the wind blew to
the shore, the fish came in

63

Charles Ricketts, vignette from Oscar Wilde's *A House of Pomegranates*,
published 1891

Charles Edward Perugini *Peonies* 1889
Oil on canvas 30½ × 23¼ in. (77·5 × 59·1 cm) Walker Art Gallery,
Liverpool
(photo, John Mills)

and Charles Hazelwood Shannon (1863–1937) are chiefly remembered for their cover designs and illustrations for Oscar Wilde's books. Their magazine *The Dial* was first issued in 1889; and the 1892 issue contained an art theory that might well be based on Albert Moore's practice of naming his pictures. This concerned Ricketts's admiration for delicate detail, or his 'theory of documents'. 'The word document,' wrote Ricketts, 'represents some exquisite detail in a masterpiece, convincing to the spectator as a thing known, yet not of necessity the symbol of a borrowed story.' Ricketts put this into practice in his illustrations for Oscar Wilde's *House of Pomegranates* (1891), where small decorative roundels are scattered, seemingly at random, among the pages, in order to evoke the atmosphere and meaning of the text.

It is perhaps possible to place a chronological limit on the Aesthetic Movement sometime in the late eighties; for Andrew Lang's witty *Ballade of Queen Anne* did just that in 1888:

> We buy her Chairs,
> Her China blue,
> Her red-brick Squares
> We build anew;
> But ah! we rue,
> When all is said,
> The tale o'er-true,
> QUEEN ANNE is dead!
>
> Friends, praise the new;
> The old is fled:
> Vivat FROU-FROU!
> QUEEN ANNE is dead!

The 1890s have for a long time been associated with art for art's sake decadence, and Lang was sensitive enough to detect at an early stage a change in the aesthetic pulse. It is, of course, still impossible to overlook Victorian society reacting to what it

Aubrey Beardsley 'How Sir Tristram drank of the Love Drink' 1893
Full page illustration in *Le Morte D'Arthur* vol. 1, facing p. 334, published by Dent, London

HOW SIR TRISTRAM
DRANK OF THE
LOVE DRINK

THE GENTLE ART

OF

MAKING ENEMIES

AS PLEASINGLY EXEMPLIFIED
IN MANY INSTANCES, WHEREIN THE SERIOUS ONES
OF THIS EARTH, CAREFULLY EXASPERATED, HAVE
BEEN PRETTILY SPURRED ON TO UNSEEMLINESS
AND INDISCRETION, WHILE OVERCOME BY AN
UNDUE SENSE OF RIGHT

LONDON MDCCCXC
WILLIAM HEINEMANN

James McNeill Whistler, title page of *The Gentle Art of Making Enemies*
1890
8 × 6 in. (20·3 × 15·2 cm) published by William Heinemann, London

Gustav Klimt, poster for the Vienna Secession Exhibition 1898
Colour lithograph $37\frac{3}{4} \times 27\frac{1}{2}$ in. (96 × 69 cm) printed by Jerlach &
Schenk, Vienna (photo, Royal Academy of Arts, Graphische Sammlung,
Albertina, Vienna)

Charles Rennie Mackintosh, Miss Cranston's Buchanan Street Tearooms,
Glasgow, c. 1897
(photo, Mackintosh Collection, University of Glasgow)
(Compare with plate on page 71)

believed was the crumbling of its moral and social institutions
when Oscar Wilde was arrested in April 1895. Naturally in
general terms Art was found to be at fault, and Aubrey Beardsley
in particular. But the emphasis on 'decadence' has long obscured
the aesthetics of the seventies and eighties which gave birth to
the art of the nineties.

Beardsley's first chance came in 1892 with his illustrations for an edition of Sir Thomas Mallory's *Morte d'Arthur* published by John Dent. The early style is a compound of Burne-Jones (who encouraged his interest in quattrocento art) fused with Japanese prints and an earnest admiration for Whistler's Peacock Room and his painting *La Princesse du Pays de la Porcelaine* which Beardsley saw there in 1891 (see page 73). For the *Morte d'Arthur*, line blocks were used rather than the more costly hand-engraved wood blocks used by Morris at the Kelmscott Press; and this was supposed to have annoyed Morris who regarded Beardsley's work as being in open competition with his own. Although always influential, Morris had long since ceased to be an innovator; and the implication of Beardsley's remark: 'while his [Morris's] work is a mere imitation of the old stuff, mine is fresh and original', gives some indication of the choice open to progressive artists of succeeding generations.

However, the stylistic criteria which governed the individual achievements of Beardsley, Morris, Whistler or Burne-Jones, were never as clear-cut to late-nineteenth-century eyes as they appear to be today; and it was these very varied manifestations of English art from about 1870 onwards which were often reinterpreted at the turn of the century by the artists of the European *Secessions*.

The potential for creating an international language, capable of being understood in terms of the twentieth century, which was not to shirk Morris's much-hated machine, was largely the responsibility of the Scottish architect and designer Charles Rennie Mackintosh (1868–1928). An Aesthetic Movement of a very individual kind arrived in Glasgow in the nineties; and it was through the magazine the *Studio* that Mackintosh enlarged a personal vision of art and nature by learning about the achievements of his English contemporaries—Beardsley and Voysey— as well as Whistler and the European Symbolist movement. Although the work of the 'Glasgow Four'—Mackintosh, his future wife Margaret Macdonald, her sister Frances and Herbert McNair—was too individual and aesthetic to arouse anything but hostility when it was shown at the Arts and Crafts exhibition in 1896, Mackintosh found instead that his designs were enthusiastically received on the Continent—in Vienna (1900), in Turin (1902) as well as in Moscow and Munich. In Austria

Charles Rennie Mackintosh, Glasgow School of Art, North Façade
1897–9 and 1907–9
(photo, Studio Seven, Glasgow)

Mackintosh's furniture was closely emulated, and his achievements
implicit in the design of Glasgow School of Art were taken up
by Josef Hoffmann and the progressive architects of the Vienna
Secession. These characteristics reappeared in a similar manner in
the buildings of Peter Behrens, thus ultimately reaching the
Bauhaus and the currency of the Modern Movement.

So too, but in a different way, was the language of twentieth-
century Expressionism intensified and enriched by Vincent Van
Gogh's familiarity with the iconography of the sunflower, which
he must surely have encountered when he lived in London in

1876. That Van Gogh, in a letter to his brother Theo written from Arles in 1888, should explicitly refer to a series of a dozen panels of sunflowers he was painting as a 'symphony in blue and yellow' further testifies to his wide knowledge of English art. In this case, it is obviously the tonal paintings of Whistler which this passage brings to mind, and which he knew. Perhaps it is appropriate that an image which Van Gogh, as an 'illustrator of the people' fervently hoped would one day hang in reproduction in the cottages of the under-privileged, should have once bloomed so luxuriantly in the London of William Morris.

Vincent Van Gogh *Sunflowers* 1888
Oil on canvas $36\frac{1}{2} \times 28\frac{1}{2}$ in. (92·7 × 72·4 cm) National Gallery, London

Selective Bibliography

All books published in London unless otherwise stated

The first 'history' of the Aesthetic Movement was Walter Hamilton *The Aesthetic Movement in England* (1882): a contemporary report mainly concerned with Pre-Raphaelite and Grosvenor Gallery artists (who were not differentiated) and 'Aesthetic' poets (including Tennyson as well as Morris and Wilde). It grudgingly admitted that the 'true Aesthetic School owed much' to Whistler. Its interest lies precisely in its indiscriminate approach. Numerous books intended for domestic consumption appeared in the 1860s and 1870s. Perhaps the most influential were C.L.Eastlake *Hints on Household Taste* (1867); Mrs H.R.Haweis *The Art of Beauty* (1878). In *The Aesthetic Movement: Prelude to Art Nouveau* (1969) Elizabeth Aslin broke entirely new ground by demonstrating how these writers—and many more—influenced the decorative arts they encouraged. Her book also contains excellent bibliographical notes, listing contemporary periodicals as well as rare and ephemeral publications. Other aspects of the Aesthetic Movement have been emphasized by various critics: Alfred J. Farmer *Le Mouvement esthétique et décadent en Angleterre: 1873–1900* (Paris 1931).

For Victorian architecture see Peter Ferriday (ed.) *Victorian Architecture* (1963); Sir Nikolaus Pevsner *Studies in Art, Architecture and Design (vol. II) Victorian and After* (1968). William Morris *Collected Works* were edited by his daughter May Morris (1910–15), and Paul Thompson *William Morris* (London/New York 1967) is the best introduction to his life and work.

For the purpose of the present study Swinburne *Essays and Studies: Some Pictures of 1868* (1874) can be supplemented by *The Swinburne Letters*, ed. Cecil Lang (New Haven 1959). Whistler published his own writings—including the 'Ten O'Clock' lecture—in *The Gentle Art of Making Enemies* (1890, with additional material 1892). The bibliography (by Elizabeth Johnston) in Andrew McLaren Young's catalogue to the Whistler exhibition organized by the Arts Council of Great Britain and the English Speaking Union of the United States (London and New

York 1960) brought up to date Don C.Seitz *Writings by and about James Abbott McNeill Whistler: A Bibliography* (Edinburgh 1910). E.R. and J.Pennell *The Life of James McNeill Whistler*, 2 vols. (Philadelphia 1908), and *The Whistler Journal* (Philadelphia 1921) remain standard source books. For Albert Moore and E.W.Godwin: A.L.Baldry *Albert Moore: His Life and Work* (1894); Dudley Harbron *The Conscious Stone: The Life of Edward William Godwin* (1949). Impressionist exhibitions in London are best documented by Douglas Cooper *The Courtauld Collection* (1954).

Some idea of the influence of Japan on Europe can be glimpsed from the following list which in no way pretends to be complete: Sir Rutherford Alcock *The Capital of the Tycoon* (1863) and *Art and Art Industries in Japan* (1878); Ernest Chesneau 'L'Art Japonais', in *Les nations rivales dans l'art* (Paris 1868); Christopher Dresser *Japan: Its Architecture, Art and Art Manufacturers* (1882; and *The Art of Decorative Design* 1862); Aimé Humbert *Le Japon Illustré*, 2 vols. (Paris 1870, English ed. 1875); J.J.Jarves *A Glimpse at the Art of Japan* (New York 1876, published serially 1869–71); Lord Redesdale (A.B.Mitford) *Tales of Old Japan* (1871, published serially in the 1860s); W.M.Rossetti *Fine Art Chiefly Contemporary* (1867, section on Japanese woodcuts published 1863).

Oscar Wilde's works were published by Robert Ross in 15 volumes (1908). For present purposes see *Miscellanies* and *Reviews*. Also *The Letters of Oscar Wilde* ed. Rupert Hart-Davis (1962); Stuart Mason (Christopher Millard) *Bibliography of Oscar Wilde* (1914).

For the illustrators: Henry Blackburn *Randolph Caldecott: His Early Art Career* (1890); Walter Crane *An Artist's Reminiscences* (1907); Leonée Ormond *George Du Maurier* (1969); H.H.Spielmann and G.S.Layard *Kate Greenaway* (1905); Gleeson White *English Illustration: The Sixties 1855-70* (1897).

For Beardsley: Brian Reade *Aubrey Beardsley* (1966) and the same author's catalogue (with Frank Dickinson) to the Beardsley Exhibition (V & A 1966); *The Letters of Aubrey Beardsley*, ed. Maas, Duncan and Good (1971). For Mackintosh: Thomas Howarth *Charles Rennie Mackintosh and the Modern Movement* (1952); Robert Macleod *Charles Rennie Mackintosh* (1968) and Andrew McLaren Young (catalogue) *Charles Rennie Mackintosh (1868–1928)—Architecture, Design and Painting* (Edinburgh 1968).

umbers in italics indicate pages containing illustrations

STUDIO VISTA | DUTTON PICTUREBACKS

edited by David Herbert